The Parents Guide to

Popular Culture

The Parents Guide to Popular Culture

By Jonathan Todd

Copyright 2011 by Jonathan Todd
All rights reserved. No part of this book may be used
or reproduced in any manner whatsoever without
written permission, except in the case of brief
quotations embodied in critical articles or reviews.
Published 2011
Printed by Createspace.com in the United States of
America

ISBN-13: 978-1456596118   ISBN-10: 145659611X

All Bible verses used were from the KJV, AKJV, ASV, BBE,
DRB, DBT, ERV, WBT, WNT, YLT, and the WEB.
All translations used are listed in the public domain.

To Steve Morris, Alex Miller, and Kendall Todd

*Your ongoing dedication to preserve your family
from the culture's corrupting influence
is an inspiration to all.*

Table of Contents

Introduction: The Situation of Our Times........…............1

1. The Prevalence of Internet Pornography……......….5

2. The Sufficiency of Scripture Concerning Magic in Entertainment Media.......................................…...13

3. The Pokémon Phenomenon............................….21

4. Can the Church Trust Disney?....................................27

5. The Sufficiency of Scripture Regarding the *Twilight Saga*...…….35

6. Who's Been Raising America's Children?................43

7. Is Music Moral or Neutral?..51

8. What In the World Is My Kid Listening To?…......57

9. Is God Against Heavy Christian Rock?....................63

10. Discerning Between "Christian Music" and Music That Truly Glorifies Christ................….......…..69

11. The Sufficiency of Scripture for Videogames......79

12. A Glance at Media as a Whole.....................…...…..85

13. The Peer Factor..................................…...95

14. Culture's Most Popular Lies......................…...103

15. Biblical Solutions......................…..........117

Introduction:
The Situation of Our Time

Today more than ever before, there is an increasing disconnection between young people and their parents. Once upon a time, a young person's life was shaped by almost nothing other than their parents and other family members. Today, that is sadly no longer a reality. Young people's lives are being shaped by two primary forces: Media and other youth. Paul Washer has even said, "America's youth are shaped by other youth, who are shaped by media." Paul Washer's insight rings true as the big picture is carefully examined. There are certain cultural lies that are sweeping away an entire generation. In an age of increased segregation and increasingly pervasive technological accessibility, America's young people are molded less and less by their parents, while being molded more and more by culture and peers. In a massive survey, 4-6 year-olds were asked to choose between watching T.V. and spending time with their fathers. 54% of the 4-6 year-olds chose T.V.![1] This and many similar developments are having a rather drastic effect on the world as we know (or don't know) it.

Josh McDowell has recently stated that from 12 to 18 months after high-school, about **95%** of high school graduates are leaving the church. Barna Research has concluded that 75% of America's teenaged youth have engaged in at least one type of psychic or witchcraft-related activity during their teen years (not including reading horoscopes).(2) Many respected surveys have proven that there is very little-to-no difference between the worldview of a "born-again Christian" teen and an unbeliever. Many surveys have proven that an extremely small percentage of parents have even a small clue of what their children are being exposed to on a regular basis from peer influence and popular culture. Terrible statistics could be read for hours, and, sadly, they are all too frighteningly real. Extremely major shifts are taking place all over America concerning its newest generation.

It is correct to say that there are multiple reasons for the sad state of the majority of young people that are growing up in this generation. This book seeks to educate parents on two of the major reasons: media and peers. The impact of cultural media has, to a large degree, captured Generation Y and isolated itself away from Generation X. The result is that parents are not aware of what their children are being exposed to and discipled by.

Peer influence has a profound effect on young people as well. This is how we invented popular rhetorical phrases like: "Well, if Tommy went to jump off a cliff, would you do that too?!" Peer influence has dramatically increased through the means of technology (texting, social media, etc.) as well as the cultural shifts that have produced increased segregation. In turn, this has increased the weight of negative peer pressure significantly. Peer influence is also a common way that mainstream media effectively beats a path toward the lives of even more young people.

Many Christian parents are unknowingly, passively, or sometimes even proactively allowing their beloved children to be exposed to many dangerous elements of this culture. This book, in no way, shape, or form, encourages the practice of legalism; however, it does strongly encourage the practice of careful discernment that is based upon knowledge of the culture as well as the Word of God. The information provided in these pages will be both enlightening and fairly shocking.

Should you find anything in these pages that you do not personally agree with, I strongly encourage you to read on. Though you may have slightly different views on some issues, there is still much more information that can benefit you and your family. Knowledge is power to make the correct decision, and it is the necessary foundation for exercising discernment. This book is designed to equip parents to deal properly with the challenges that are facing them in this unique time in history.

Please continue to keep in mind that most of these things are just "extensions of the heart". Yes, it is important to be aware of these things and to deal with these things; however, we must make sure to always address any underlying heart issues that may have helped these things become an issue. Sometimes, it is a case of mere ignorance. Other times, it is a deep-seated, intense spiritual condition that must be properly dealt with. In any case, this book will be of great help in taking the first several steps in dealing with them.

It is my hope that the Holy Spirit will use this information to stimulate your family toward a stronger faith, an increased holiness, and a separation from the corruption of the world that begins in the heart and gradually moves outward in a believer's style of life. May God now prepare your heart to receive the well-documented truth concerning the American pop-culture of the 21st century.

Chapter 1
The Prevalence of Internet Pornography

Pornography: We all know what it is, yet many parents are not aware of *the* most common way that it is accidentally stumbled across by young people. On *today's* internet, one does not have to seek out pornography in order to be exposed to it. Pornography advertisers have developed programs, systems, and technology that effectively seek out the internet user. Many of these systems have been designed to primarily seek out children and young adults. This is largely because these advertisers know that if they can entrap people while they are young, they will probably have them trapped for the majority of their lives. Many times, once a young person has been exposed to pornography, they will return to it in order to see more; then, the addiction cycle has been commenced. The purpose of this chapter is to give parents insight as to what takes place to provide this unwanted exposure, how prevailing the problem is today, and some possible solutions to this common problem.

First, it is helpful to clearly perceive that

Christian adults are very vulnerable to this struggle, so how much more so would the average Christian youth or child be vulnerable? All of the following survey results are from multiple respected organizations in order to provide realistic results.

- 50% of all professing Christian men and 20% of all professing Christian women are addicted to porn.(1)

- Over 50% of pastors say cyber-porn is a possible temptation.(2)

- Almost 40% of pastors say that porn is a current struggle.(3)

- Another survey found that 40% of pastors had intentionally visited a porn site.(4)

- 47% of Christians are actually aware that pornography is a problem in the home.(5)

> "The heart is deceitful above all things, and desperately wicked: who can know it?"
> Jeremiah 17:9

"Porn has become a major presence in the lives of youth, and while the majority of parents have expressed concern about sexual content, few parents are consistently supervising internet usage or using available technology to block sexual content."(6) Too many Christian parents deceive themselves by imagining that their child would never do such a thing. The small minority of parents that are actually correct still need to seriously consider the common factor of unwanted (accidental) exposure. Such factors are outlined in the following statistics:

- Less than 7% of parents know all of what their child is accessing on the internet.(7)

- **Average age** of first internet exposure to pornography is **11** years old.(8)

- Over 40% of 10-17 year-olds admitted to viewing online pornography just in the last 12 months. Of those, **over 65% did not want to view the images and had not sought them out.**(9)

- **90% of children aged 8-16** have viewed pornography on the Internet at some time. In most cases, the sex sites were accessed **unintentionally** when a child, often in the process of doing homework, used a **seemingly innocent sounding word to search for information or pictures**.(10)

- **93%** of Americans, aged **12-17**, use the internet.(11) Coincidentally, the **largest** consumer of internet pornography is the **12-17** age group.(12)

- 1 in 5 children (10-17 years old) receives unwanted sexual solicitations online.(13)

- 43% of children internet users have openly admitted to closing or minimizing the browser at the first sound of a parental step.(14)

- Over 60% of teens claimed to know how to hide what they do online from their parents. Many of them have private email addresses or private social networking profiles to effectively conceal what they do online.(15)

- 30% of teenage girls polled by the Girl Scout Research Institute said that they had been sexually harassed in a chat-room.(16)

- Only 7% of the sexually harassed girls told their parents. The rest were too worried that their parents would ban them from going online.(17)

- 86% of the girls polled said that they could chat online without their parents' knowledge, and 54% of them could even conduct a cyber-relationship.[18]

- 90% of males and 70% of females (aged 13-14) in Alberta, Canada reported accessing sexually-explicit media content at least once.[19]

- The main concern for parents has shifted from television to the Internet; 85% of parents say that it poses the greatest risk to their children among all forms of media.[20]

"There has never before, in the history of telecommunications media in the United States, been so much indecent (and obscene) material that is so easily accessible by so many minors in so many American homes with so few restrictions."
U.S. Department of Justice [21]

Many parents believe that it is safe to allow their children to have a Facebook account. They do not realize that Facebook has made it into many headlines because of their inability to stop pornography from being posted all over their website. Pornography businesses design fake profiles with explicit (or sexually-suggestive) pictures and will begin sending friend requests to thousands upon thousands of random people. I have personally received seven of these friend invitations just in the last two months.

Porn advertisers will also purchase an ad spot on Facebook and post up their pornography ads; meanwhile, Facebook does not catch it. I've personally watched two 10 year-olds (both from Christian homes) staring at a near-naked pornographic ad on Facebook. They both quickly became visibly upset at me when I told them to get rid of it.

Porn advertisers also make seemingly innocent profiles and begin posting up pornography ads and photos on fan pages and profiles for all to see. Facebook, MySpace, YouTube, children's online gaming sites, and many other assumed "safe sites" are not truly safe from the pervasive plague of online pornography.

There is no excuse for giving a child over to sexual perversion just because one is lazy or not cautious enough. The book of Proverbs condemns the popular practice of parenting with a slack hand. A parent should be preserving their child; they should be actively protecting them from moral corruption. Sadly, this is getting more difficult as time goes on. However, we must not "grow weary in well doing". (Galatians 6:9)

I have included a few possible solutions that should be acted upon if **personally** monitoring your child's internet usage is not an option. All internet usage should obviously be

completely necessary, and the best form of monitoring is "over the shoulder". It is senseless to let them be online without a very good reason. It is even more senseless not to have some effective way of monitoring internet consumption.

Covenant Eyes is, by far, the best program for accountability and/or internet filtering. Its accountability system stores all browser history, shows what times the internet was used, and can even deny the internet from being used after a predetermined amount of time of usage or time of day. The information and control is made available to the parents. For those services, as well as others, is a charge of $8.99/mo. They also offer internet filtering (which will block unintentional access) for $4.99/mo. A cheaper option is Webchaver. It is affiliated with Covenant Eyes and offers accountability for just $3.99/mo. It also offers filtering for only $1.99/mo. I personally use Webchaver's accountability program and have found it to be very easy to use. The services are very beneficial, and the customer service is very responsive and helpful.

God has provided ways to protect your child for $2 - $14 a month. Is your child's purity worth that investment? You wouldn't hand your child a loaded gun. Why give them something that has proven to be spiritually dangerous if the proper per-cautionary measures are not in place? Both Covenant Eyes and Webchaver can be reached toll free at 1-877-479-1119. Their websites can be found at covenanteyes.com and webchaver.org, respectively.

(I am not affiliated with Covenant Eyes in any way. I am merely a very satisfied customer who chose them after research of multiple accountability and filtering products.)

Chapter 2
The Sufficiency of Scripture Concerning Magic in Entertainment Media:

Magic has long been a common thread of all civilizations. It eventually found its way into Hollywood and has since introduced a new flourishing debate among many Christian circles. There is much controversy and lack of knowledge concerning the role of magic or "fantasy magic" in a Christian's entertainment choices. Is *any* magic in media entertainment appropriate for the Christian? And if so, is it all magic, or does it depend on the context? As most of us know, the Bible mentions magic quite frequently. However, what the Bible does *not ever do* is depict magic as being acceptable or neutral. Today many films that are being accepted by Christian audiences portray magic in a way that is against Scripture. In order to understand this, we must first be aware of the belief system that exists in the world of paganism. Once we are equipped with this knowledge, we can then examine some examples and seek the sufficiency of Scripture.

The standard pagan belief system says that there is one universal "force" that is available to be tapped into by both the "good" and the "bad" side. The belief is that magic, in of itself, is entirely neutral. Some use it for good (classified as white magic) and some use it for selfish gain (classified as black magic.) We all have probably seen this very belief system being portrayed in *Star Wars* among many others. We witnessed this belief system being portrayed in *The Wizard of Oz*. There is the "Wicked Witch of the West" and the "Good Witch of the North". The problem remains that the Bible says that there are no "good witches" and no "neutral magic". Paganism says that there is. Revelations says three times that the people who do not repent of sorcery and magic arts will be afflicted and thrown into hell.

While it is true that magic is acceptable in **a strictly fantasy sense** (wherein the said "magic" has **absolutely NO correlation** with real magic*), hardly anyone even knows how to tell the difference… Especially not a child!* If a Christian is not ready to ban it altogether, then they must be capable of distinguishing between the portrayal of real magic and fantasy magic. If one has enough knowledge to make an accurate discernment, they find that almost 100% of the magic in the entertainment industry has direct correlations with real magic. Aside from that, let us now dig deeper into this "less than enchanting" dis-agreement between Christians.

The Wizard of Oz:

Baum, the occultist who authored *The Wizard of Oz* and converted it into a stage play before it became one of the most popular movies of all time, claimed, "There is a **strong tendency** in modern novelists toward introducing some vein of **mysticism** or **occultism** into their writings." Baum also claimed that he was a medium for Satan, and that he had **channeled** *The Wizard of Oz* as a result.[1] *The Wizard of Oz* taught that it's not necessary to seek God because we have the necessary power within: meditation, incantations, contemplative prayer, etc.

Harry Potter:

The naïve, Christian-based arguments for the *Harry Potter* series are usually, "Well, it's just fantasy." My question is, "Is that really so?" The storyline is not based upon a true story, but the witchcraft taking place in the story does indeed take place in real life. Divination, numerology, astrology, clairvoyance, astral projection, and the like are all real parts of the Satanic and pagan lifestyle; this is where discernment should come into play.

Jeremiah Films has stated, "Harry's world says that drinking dead animal blood gives power, a satanic human sacrifice and Harry's powerful blood brings new life, demon possession is not spiritually dangerous, and that passing through fire, contacting the dead, and conversing with ghosts and others in the spirit world, and more, is normal and acceptable."(8)

MTV News has stated, "A surprising number of young witches *MTV News* spoke with also said that they became curious about their **faith** through misguiding pop-culture fare like *The Craft* and the *Harry Potter* series." *MTV* also admitted, "Guess a few conservative Christian groups were right about that one."(4)

A study has been published by the *New York Times* that named Wicca as "the fastest growing religion in America".(5) By the year 2012, it is estimated to become America's **third-largest** religion, as the number of adherents continues to double every 30 months.(6)

The Lord of the Rings:

At this point in time, it is hard for me to *authoritatively* say whether *LOTR* is a biblical abomination or not. So instead of possibly misrepresenting God's Word one way or the other, I will simply list many cautions that need to be considered concerning the *LOTR* series.

First of all, we must realize that if we allow children to view the supernatural events that are in *LOTR*, it will most likely confuse them about why *LOTR* is acceptable while other movies that show the supernatural are not acceptable. This is because the supernatural elements that are presented in the movie imitate witchcraft. Gandalf frequently participates in activities such as scrying, casting spells with incantations, sorcery, controlling animals, etc. It should be considered potentially dangerous to present these things as being acceptable to a child. It will potentially damage their spiritual discernment, as well as help develop their appetite towards being entertained by (and in some cases, to participating in) the occult. We know that the world is becoming more and more interested in the occult. Revelations says that the antichrist will cause the craft to prosper in his hand. This means that it will continue to get more popular, and we must all be very careful in dealing with this issue.

We must also be careful that we are fleeing the very appearance of evil (1 Thessalonians 5:22). Nor do we wish and to call anything good that is actually evil (Isaiah 5:20).

It is true that Tolkien had a deep interest in pagan mythology. The very idea of there being "lesser gods" links back to that. This is where he got many of the characters for the story as well (such as Gandalf). We must be very careful with *potentially* mixing darkness with light. **"And what agreement hath the temple of God with idols."** 2

Corinthians 6:16 May the Holy Spirit lead you in this.

I am not completely sure whether God commands it as being unacceptable for every believer or not. My indecision lies within multiple factors that I do not have the space to thoroughly address. However, I would never expect a child to understand what the line is. I have studied it for many hours, and I still am not sure where it falls. How could I expect a child to discern the difference between the acceptable and unacceptable? Whether it is abominable or not, there are clearly many cautions that should be taken into thoughtful, deliberate consideration.

Is white witchcraft acceptable for the Christian audience?

The *Satanic Bible* says that there is no real difference between white and black magic. It states, "White magic is supposedly utilized only for good or un-selfish purposes, and black magic, we are told, is used only for selfish or evil reasons. Satanism draws no such dividing line." The author also stated, "There is no difference between 'white' and 'black' magic, except in the smug hypocrisy, guilt-ridden righteousness, and self-deceit of the 'white' magician himself."[2]

God's Word is *saturated* with categorical warnings against **all** forms of the occult. This includes astrology (horoscopes), contacting the dead, sorcery, divination, and witchcraft. (Ex. 22:18; Lev. 19:26, 31, 20:6, 27; Deut. 18:10-12; 1 Sam. 15:23a; 2 Kings 21:6, 23:24; I Chron. 10:13; Isa. 2:6, 8:19-20, 19:3, 47: 12-14; Ez. 13:20-23; Daniel 2:27-28; Mal. 3:5; Acts 13:8-11, 16:16-18, 19:19; Gal. 5:19-20; Rev 9:19-21, 21:8, 22:15, etc.)

"By disassociating magic from supernatural evil, it becomes possible to portray occult practices as being somehow 'good' and 'healthy', contrary to the scriptural declaration that such practices are 'detestable to the Lord'. This, in turn, opens the door for kids to become fascinated with the supernatural while tragically failing to seek or recognize the one true source of supernatural good: namely God."[3]

Antinomianism is a doctrine that is defined as, "The doctrine or belief that the Gospel **frees Christians from required obedience to any law, whether scriptural**, civil, or **moral**, and that salvation is attained solely through faith and the gift of divine grace."[7] Many Scriptures could be properly used to prove the errors in that doctrine, but one verse from James is more than sufficient: **"Faith without works is no faith at all."**

Things that are clearly inappropriate to participate in, are also wrong to find amusement and entertainment from. This book is filled with verses about how the *very idea* of evil should be treated. "Casting down imaginations, and every high thing that exalteth itself against the knowledge of God, and bringing into captivity every thought to the obedience of Christ." 2 Corinthians 10:5

The bottom line is this: God has labeled sorcery, witchcraft, and the like as being detestable abominations. It would be correct to say that he does not find abominations as being entertaining; God indeed despises them. If a Christian wants it in their entertainment, certain knowledge is required of them: the knowledge that enables one to discern whether the magic taking place has <u>any</u> correlation with real magic, or whether it is <u>strictly</u> fantasy magic.

"Blessed are those who wash their robes clean… and may go through the gates into the city. **The unclean are shut out**, and ***so are all who practice magic***…"
Revelation 22:14-15a

"Stand now with thine **enchantments**, and with the multitude of thy **sorceries**…let now the **astrologers**… stand up, and save thee. Behold, they shall be as stubble**; the fire shall burn them**;"
Isaiah 47:12a, 13b, 14b

The fear of the LORD is to hate evil. Proverbs 8:13

Chapter 3
The Pokémon Phenomenon

Pokémon has been the largest children's phenomenon in the past 15 years and has officially taken America by storm. According to Google, Pokémon is googled more than 980,000 times every single day in America.[1] That's over 40,000 times every single hour in America! There are *Pokémon* video games, collectible cards, toys, clothing, a TV show, and more. Pokémon has stolen many children's hearts, many teenagers' free time, and many parents' resources. The purpose of this chapter is to present information that is sadly not well-known in the Christian community. There are many things that could be discussed on this topic, but because of limited space, this information will attempt to be brief and concise.

First off, *Pokémon* was published by Wizards of The Coast. That same company has also published *Magic: the Gathering* and *Dungeons and Dragons*. Later, Hasbro purchased Wizards of the Coast and also **began marketing Ouija boards to children**. Pagan and satanic themes are very rampant in these games mentioned. Any witch would easily recognize them to be instruction in entry-level witchcraft. The teachings range from summoning demons, to satanic rituals, to accomplishing acts of sorcery. Compared to the other games though, *Pokémon* has proven to be the most subtle and has seemingly snuck into the Christian community more effectively. Scripture clearly defines *Pokémon* as anti-Christ for its heavy use of witchcraft, sorcery, black magic, and its pagan and Satanic belief systems. Please allow me to elaborate from a Biblical standpoint.

Witchcraft, sorcery, and black magic:

What are the pokemon's purposes, and how do they seek to accomplish these common purposes? Pokémon are summoned to do battle and to protect through violent and supernatural means. This is the very equivalent of sorcery.

The following are some of the attacks (taken straight from witchcraft and black magic) that are available to the psychic and elemental types of pokemon: *cosmic power, hypnosis, imprison, kinesis, psychic, teleport, telekinesis, meditate, mind reader, magic coat, future sight (divination), curse, earth power, energy ball, magical leaf, and sacred fire.* These are words that one could read on a psychic's store-front window or in a book that instructs in witchcraft.

Let us now consider just a few of the pokemon. They are among the most powerful pokemon: *Abra* and *Kadabra*. These are among the psychic type, and one actually evolves into the other. Abra evolves into Kadabra upon gaining enough power.

It is interesting that Abra + Kadabra = *Abracadabra*. *Webster's Dictionary* defines the word in this way. 1) "A word supposed to have magic powers and hence used in incantations, on amulets, etc." 2) "A magic spell or formula." It is listed as a word under sorcery. The *American Heritage Dictionary* states, "...Abracadabra was a magic word..." Eventually, Abra can turn into *Alakazam* (another magic word associated with the occult.)

On the Abra card we read, "Using its *ability to read minds*, it will identify impending danger and *teleport* to safety." Kadabra even has a pentagram on his forehead and an SSS on his chest. Both of these symbols have strong occult significance. It is clear from the Bible that Christians are not to participate or associate with activities related to the occult.

Is it a mere accident or perhaps some weird coincidence that these words of the occult were used in this game to describe characters that perform various kinds of sorcery and black magic?

I pray that no real Christian would be so naïve (or spiritually deceived) enough to think so.

Pagan/Satanic Belief Systems:

Buddhist Mysticism, Hinduism, Evolution, *Egyptian Book of the Dead, Book of Tao, The Analects of Confucius, The Gita, The I Ching,* and *The Tibetan Book of the Dead* have all influenced and played a part in the creation of *Pokémon.* *Pokémon* echoes every type of paganism by heavily incorporating the four elements (*earth, fire, wind, water*) in the exact same ways that Wicca and other pagan religions do. *Pokémon* even incorporates the pentagram. The pentagram is a standard pagan and satanic symbol used to illustrate the four basic elements plus a pantheistic spiritual being: such as Gaia or Mother Earth. So basically, the same themes that are present in every single demonic religion (from Wicca to Satanism) are used *extensively* in the *Pokémon* game, movie, cards, and T.V. show.

Now to dig deeper, we will look into the story-line of the cartoon. Ash, the hero of the series, goes to a tower that is haunted by dead pokemon; Ash wishes to detect and identify them (spirit communication). While in the tower, Ash is attacked by Channelers; they are described as possessed people who use dead pokemon to attack live pokemon (necromancy). In the story, one

Channeler even chants, "Give me your soul... Give me your soul." He chants this phrase over and over again.(2) Channelers are people who channel; they become possessed with a spirit who communicates through the human host. This encounter with the occult, as well as others in the story-line, is specifically selected for a pre-teen audience.

At another point of the story, Bill, a pokemon researcher, confidently states that the earth is 4.6 billion years old... This is exactly what children are told in the fable of macro-evolution! There is also an incident where Ash (who children role-play throughout the game) allows his spirit to be taken out of his body by Haunter.(3) This practice is called *astral projection* and is common in the realm of paganism. It's interesting that Haunter is the one that assists Ash in astral projection because it is necessary (in these demonic practices) to have a demon spirit **reside** in one's body while they take their spirit out (hence the name "Haunter"). Clearly this is instance upon instance of *children* being subtly indoctrinated with the occult.

None of this pagan/satanic material was placed into the game by mistake, and there is much more where that came from. *Pokémon* is actually a *minor* case of this compared to many other games on the market today: *Yu-Gi-Oh*,

Dungeons and Dragons, *World of Warcraft*, *Runescape*, and *Magic: The Gathering* just to name a few. Many Christian children are being discipled by occultism and demonism through the medium of entertainment. Numerous Christian schools and families have caught onto these truths and have made news' headlines by personally banning Pokémon and other witchcraft paraphernalia. Sadly, many other Christian families have not been as careful as was needed and have unknowingly given Satan ground in their homes and lives.

"Finally, brothers, whatever things are true, whatever things are honest, whatever things are just, whatever things are pure, whatever things are lovely, whatever things are of good report; if there be any virtue, and if there be any praise, think on these things." Philippians 4:8

"Be haters of what is evil; keep your minds fixed on what is good." Romans 12:9b

"Many of those who practiced magical arts brought their books together and burned them in the sight of all. They counted the price of them, and found it to be fifty thousand pieces of silver." Acts 19:19

"But I wish you to be wise as to what is good, and simple-minded as to what is evil." Romans 16:19b

"Neither shall you bring an abomination into your house, lest you be a cursed thing like it:" Duet. 7:26

Chapter 4
Can The Church Trust Disney?

For many years Disney has all but monopolized the entertainment industry. Consumers usually speak highly of Disney and are pleased to support them. Many Christians allow their children to watch Disney movies, personally visit "The Magic Kingdom," and even defend Disney as being wholesome entertainment. Unfortunately, there is a great deal of information that the average Christian is not aware of or perhaps has just not properly considered. There are two agendas in particular that especially need to be exposed to the Christians that are still unaware: the sexual and homosexual agenda and the occult/anti-Christ agenda. Awareness of these things is critical because a Christian would not want to partake in, or support in any way, such detestable abominations.

The Sexual and Homosexual Agenda:

The *Washington Times* recorded Disney **actively** opposing the Child Online Protection Act (COLPA) which would restrict child pornography material on the Internet.[1]

The AFA's monitoring has revealed that Disney has been one of the **top sponsors** of pro-homosexual TV programming.(2)

Disney president, Michael Eisner, is quoted as saying that he thinks **40%** of Disney's 63,000 employees are homosexual.(3)

Disney-**owned** Miramax released the homosexual movie, *Lie down with Dogs*.(4)

Chicks in White Satin is a film about a lesbian couple who decide on a semi-traditional "commitment celebration".(5)

Color of Night shows co-stars, Bruce Willis and Jane March, entwined in numerous sex scenes that feature full-frontal nudity.(6)

The Disney Star, Miley Cyrus, (aka *Hannah Montana*) was recently photographed "nude" in a "bedroom environment" in *Vanity Fair* magazine. What Christian would still think that she is a good role model? She is subject to other people's decision making.

Kids was described by *Variety Magazine* as "one of the most controversial American movies ever made." According to *Newsweek*, "The film follows a number of barely pubescent-looking boys and girls around New York City as they smoke pot, bait gays, beat a black man, and engage in graphic sex." Under pressure by the public eye, Disney formed an independent company to market and distribute the [child] pornographic movie.(7)

Disney hired Lauren Lloyd, a self-avowed lesbian, for the development of lesbian movies. *Out Magazine*, a homosexual publication, praised Disney, "...lesbians are not yet chic entertainment attractions for a lot of America. With **Lloyd** and **Disney** on our side though, anything is possible." (8)

In June, 1996, Disney promoted the 6th annual **"Gay and Lesbian Day at Walt Disney World."** Disney even portrayed Mickey Mouse and Donald Duck as homosexual partners. Minnie Mouse and Daisy Duck were portrayed as lesbians.

On March 19, *ABC* (which is owned and controlled by Disney) aired a show that portrayed George Washington doing cocaine and Ben Franklin in bed with a man.

Disney considered buying *Ripe*, a movie about the deflowering of 14-year-old twins.(9)

Actors, Ernie Sabella and Nathan Lane, said in a *New York Times* interview that the characters they played (Timon and Pumbaa) in *The Lion King* are "the first homosexual Disney characters ever to come to the screen...."(11)

A Disney-**owned** subsidiary has published *Lettin' It All Hang Out*, (the autobiography of RuPaul, a well-known transvestite entertainer) and *Growing up Gay*, (written by three homosexual comedians who targeted "gay youngsters bred by heterosexuals" as their audience.)

It should be noted that Disney has created many different companies for itself so that it can put out "adult" content without damaging its reputation in the public eye. Many Christians have fallen for this clever, deceptive business strategy.

The Occult/Anti-Christ Agenda:

Disney has continuously put out more and more movies that have blatant pagan elements. This is especially true considering these recent years. The following are just a few examples:

- In *Misadventures of Merlin Jones* (1964), a genius dabbles in hypnotism & ESP.
- In *Bednobs & Broomsticks* (1971), a witch finds a magic formula. The magic formula raises a ghostly army (necromancy).
- In *Child of Glass* (1978), a glass doll must be found to set a ghost free in a haunted house.
- In *Beyond Witch Mountain* (1982), a pair of twins has to use their special occult powers to outwit a character named Deranian.
- In *The Black Cauldron* (1985), a Horned King uses his magic to fight a clairvoyant pig and the pig's keeper.
- In *Bride of Boogedy* (1987), an evil spirit visits the Davis family and puts the father under a spell.
- *Aladdin* (1992) features an all-powerful genie and, of course, occult teachings are spread throughout the movie.
- In *Pocahontas* (1995), Disney promoted pantheism and censored out the historical fact that Pocahontas converted from paganism to Christianity.
- *Hercules* (1997) is completely based-off of pagan mythology.
- *Mulan* (1998) portrayed ancestor worship and demonic spirit assistance.

- *Dogma* (1999) attacks Christianity by cleverly asserting over and over that Christian beliefs are mere Christian mythology.(10)
- *The Haunted Mansion* (2003) includes things such as demons, a crystal ball, spirits, attempted suicide, and more.
- *The Princess and the Frog* (2010) features both an "evil scheming voodoo magician" and a "good voodoo queen." This is the lie of Wicca/white magic.

A Walt Disney press release let it be known that Disney would be bringing Danzig, a satanic band, into their record company. According to Disney, their first music album, Black Acid Devil, has "dark, Gothic, and sexual" overtones. Danzig has also released an album titled "**Deth Red Saboath**" which celebrates Christ's death as the victory of Satan and Satan's forces.

On *ABC Family* (that is owned and controlled by Disney) December 4th's weekend (2010) is being promoted as the *"Harry Potter* Weekend."

Disney has purchased the rights to play T.V. shows like *Grey's Anatomy* and *Desperate Housewives*. *ABC*, being owned by Disney, has, of course, propagated this blasphemy and filth such as follows:

- A young patient, Justin, requires a new heart but feels guilty that another child had to die. A priest tells Justin, "God wants you to live. That's why He sent you the heart. Justin replies, "**I'm not <u>stupid</u>, okay? God didn't send me the heart. There's no such thing as God**." (*ABC*, ***Grey's Anatomy***, December 11, 2005)

- Gabi has had sex with teenager John. John tells her: "Me and my friend Justin had this bet to see who could **lose their virginity first this summer at <u>Bible camp</u>**. Guess I beat him to the punch." (*ABC*, ***Desperate Housewives***, May 21, 2006)

- Dwight asks Shirley to represent him in a divorce, stating that he committed **bestiality** by having sex with a cow: "It's not what you think… **I've been a good husband for 23 years. I'm a <u>deacon</u> at our church!**" (*ABC*, ***Boston Legal***, November 8, 2005)

- Freddie talks about his sister's list of 'Things to Do Before I Go to College:' "There was a big check next to '**Lose**

> **Virginity'**. It was right between 'Make Sexy Mix Tape' and '**Apologize to Christ**'." (*ABC*, ***Freddie***, October 19, 2005)

Satan has been deceiving Christians to support, and even defend, the propagation of this detestable filth. Many Christians have also been indoctrinated with world-views that are not at all compatible with Scripture.

According to the book, *Satanism in America*, hardcore Satanism is "the fastest-growing subculture among America's TEENS." According to Kinsey, 28% of boys and 17% of girls have one or more **same-sex** experiences **before age 20** and about 50% teens have sex in high school. Why would we want to help inflate these statistics by supporting a company that so effectively promotes and funds the propagation of such abominations!? Many "Christians," even after all this information, will *still* try to defend their favorite movies because the enemy has stolen their heart and affections. Let us do what each of us deems necessary in order to "have nothing to do with the barren unprofitable deeds of darkness, but, instead of that, set your faces against them." Ephesians 5:11

> "Who will rise up for me against the evildoers? [Or] who will stand up for me against the workers of iniquity?" Psalms 94:16

Chapter 5
The Sufficiency of Scripture Regarding the *Twilight Saga*

There is much debate in Christian circles over a popular new series: *The Twilight Saga*. As the Church responds to this series in various ways, Christians are being accused by one another of being everything from delusional, to legalistic, to spiritually deceived. 1 Corinthians 2:15a says, "But he that is spiritual judgeth all things." People are definitely making judgments, but what some people lack is their foundation on which to make such judgments. It should always be the very Word of God instead of personal perspective and mere fickle emotion. The following is a brief discernment of the nature, elements, author, and the fruit of the *Twilight* saga from the foundation of God's Word.

First of all, one must understand that vampirism is **not** fictional. It is a subculture that has existed for over a thousand years and has recently been becoming much more mainstream. There are numerous testimonies of ex-witches and ex-Satanists who say that vampirism is a real (and thriving) practice. There are many nonfictional, historical accounts from the Romans, Egyptians (who took very meticulous records), and Africans that all concur. Vampirism was well-known on local and international levels by the arrival of the Middle Ages. In today's time period, the only people that regularly drink blood from humans and animals are pagans and Satanists. As one progresses to the higher levels of Satanism and witchcraft, they are forced to drink animal and human blood more and more in order to keep their strength and to gain/maintain their demonic power.

Leviticus 17:14 teaches us that life is in the blood. Satan wants to destroy and consume life. For many centuries, people have been drinking blood to appease the forces of darkness. **Today vampirism is recognized as a religion by all pagans and the very church of Satan.** Drinking blood and blood sacrifice is an **everyday reality** for occultists all over the world. The Bible says that blood is sacred, and that drinking it is an abomination; it also correlates drinking blood with idol worship and witchcraft. So right off the bat, we see that *Twilight* is effectively trivializing a very present, dark evil.

The basic storyline of the *Twilight Saga* is as follows: Bella falls in love with Edward, who is a vampire, who lives in a coven of 13 vampires. (The word *coven* belongs to Wiccan terminology and means *13 witches*; *13* is the number for rebellion.) Edward emphatically believes that he is damned to hell because he is a vampire. He repeatedly warns Bella not to join him in his vampirism because of the eternal damnation that she will surely face, but she <u>eagerly chooses</u> eternal separation from God for being able to be a vampire with him. She even treats the grave reality of hell in a very flippant manner. Quote, "I decided that as long as I'm going to hell, I might as well do it thoroughly." At one point, Edward asks Bella, "So eager for eternal damnation?" He quickly receives an affirmative response. For a Christian to rationalize this kind of evil is to submerge one's self into the mire of relative truth and lack of reverence for all that is holy, pure, and true.

Here are a few (out of many) things that are clearly in direct opposition with God's perfect will, character, nature, and Word.

- Bella mocks God's purposes in creation when she proudly states, "I was born to be a vampire."
- Edward encourages Bella multiple times to deceive her father; she "quite virtuously" complies.
- Bella states that marriage is "stupid" and husbands are "dull". This is blasphemy

against God (the Creator of marriage and family) and His design.
- The *salvation by works* doctrine is present throughout the story. This is consistent with Stephanie Meyer's Mormonism. Christ's saving power is also denied.
- Bella says, "Children, in the abstract, had never appealed to me. They seemed to be loud creatures, often dripping some form of goo." The Bible says well over 30 times that children are a blessing from the LORD.
- Deuteronomy 18:9-12 condemns divination, sorcery, interpreting omens, engaging in witchcraft, casting spells, being a medium or spiritist, and consulting the dead. That list covers every supernatural element in the story: mind reading, levitation, lycanthropy (shape shifting), pre-cognitive knowledge of future events (medium-ship), and other various supernatural strengths.

Many red-flags appear when the author, Stephanie Meyer, is considered. First of all, she is a Mormon and is quoted saying that she is "against humanity". This view manifests itself in the story when Bella calls her former human face "hideous" and refers to her new vampire face as being "glorious". God's design of a human face is not hideous! What's more, a corruption of God's design could never be properly considered "glorious"!

Meyer states that much of her inspiration, in writing her vampire saga, came from a band of musicians called Marjorie Fair. Meyer gushes, "For *New Moon*, they were absolutely essential. They can put you into a **suicidal state** faster than anything I know." And, "Their songs really made it [**death**] beautiful for me."[1] She also said that My Chemical Romance (another popular band) was her inspiration for a character in the story.[2] My Chemical Romance has songs about drinking blood, committing suicide, doing drugs... Do you get the picture?

Stephanie Meyer has written portions of *Prom Nights from Hell*. It is about supernatural events surrounding evil prom nights. She has also written an adult novel about "invading souls" that take over a person and get the person to do whatever they so desire... **News Flash --** That behavior is called demonic possession! Meyer's occult philosophy continues to get more and more blatant as our study of her persists.

Christ stated that we can know a tree by its fruit. So let's have a quick examination of some of the apple orchard, shall we?

Typical Twilight fan site -
Twilight Children: "Wicca online community for Pagans and Wiccans"
wiccantogether.com/group/twilightchildren

T-shirts marketed to young girls -

- "Bite me, Please."
- "Save gas, ride a vampire."
- "Edward broke my headboard."
- "Only vampires love you forever."
- "Roses are red, and violets are blue, let me sink my teeth into you."

"Edward's" words in an interview -

Interviewer – "Is it weird to have girls that are so young have this incredibly sexualized thing around you?"

"Edward" replies, "It's weird that you get **eight-year-old girls** coming up to you saying, 'Can you just bite me? I want you to bite me.' It is really strange how young the girls are..." [Laughs](3)

Almost every single fruit, that I've seen, is directly connected to either sexual lust for Jacob or Edward, witchcraft, or all three! Is this really surprising though? Take into account that there are pages and pages of text that are first-person accounts of Bella's sexual encounters with Edward. They describe, in detail, the feelings, the caresses, buttons being unbuttoned, etc. Should any of this really be a surprise? Meyer is in a demonic false religion! According to 2 Timothy 2:26, she has been taken captive to do Satan's will!

It is shocking to see all of the self-professing Christians that attempt to rationalize all this wickedness away. Truth is not relative! As previously stated, the fastest-growing subculture among America's **teens is Satanism**. I urge every self-professing Christian that is reading this to "clothe yourselves with Jesus Christ." (Romans 13:14)

"That no advantage may be gained over us by Satan: for we are not ignorant of his devices."
1 Corinthians 2:11

"Woe unto them who call evil good, and good evil; who put darkness for light, and light for darkness; who put bitter for sweet, and sweet for bitter!"
Isaiah 5:20

Chapter 6
Who's Been Raising America's Children?

The last few decades have seen no parallel in world history concerning the prevalence of heavy media exposure and saturation into one, single generation. We are in the midst of an enormous social experiment. This experiment is determining the final outcome of the generation that has thoroughly been engrossed by it. Television alone has been quoted as being the single biggest director of culture in America from 1960 to now. The various number arrangements that convey the media's influence, power, audience, and usage continue to steeply increase. Our current situation is very unique, and the playing field has been stacked against the Christian. The detrimental impacts have proven to be a handicap on the church and our society. Biblical solutions are necessities that urgently need to be carefully considered and very quickly implemented.

The Situation:

99% of American households have a TV set.[1]

54% of kids have a TV in their own bedroom.(2)

81% of children between ages 2 and 7 watch TV alone and unsupervised. That jumps up to 95% for ages 7 and up.(3)

44% of kids say they watch something different when they're alone than with their parents (25% choose MTV).(4)

The average media use per day is **7 hours and 38 minutes**. That's over **15 years** of one's life (if they live to life expectancy.) TV accounts for more than half of that figure.(5)

Time spent in "meaningful conversation" with parents -- a mere 3.5 minutes per day.(6)

The average American youth spends more time on the TV than they do on their entire high school education.(7)

By age 18, a child will, on average, have witnessed 200,000-250,000 acts of violence, including 18,000 murders.(8)

> "Children see more sin in a month then their grandparents, or their great grandparents, probably saw in their entire lifetime."
> John MacArthur

The Playing Field:

Every single popular children's network has released shows that include witchcraft, disrespect to authority, situational ethics, improper humor, rebellion, and indecent behavior. Why do these children networks allow such material to be discipling children?

- ***Nickelodeon*** is owned by the same company that owns *MTV*. Research has proven that after just 1 hour of *MTV*, adolescents are much more likely to approve of premarital sex.(9)

- ***Disney*** is on a trend of putting out homosexual, godless media material, and they actively promote many other abominations as well.

- The owners of the ***Cartoon Network*** also own *Adult Swim*: the youth/adult cartoon network that is filled with sex, drugs, and blasphemy aimed straight at the Lord Jesus Christ.

- ***Fox Kids*** is owned by the **Fox Entertainment Group.** *Family Guy, That 70's Show, The Simpsons, American Dad,* and other wickedness frequent their playlist.

A study was done on the Family Hour: the most "family-friendly" hour of television programming. In **180 hours** of original programming, there were **2246** instances of objectionable, violent, profane, and sexual content. This resulted in an average of **12.48 instances per television hour, or <u>one instance every 4.8 minutes</u>.** This study analyzed *ABC, CBS, Fox, NBC, CW,* and *My Network TV.*(10)

"I will set no vile thing before my eyes. I hate the deeds of faithless men. They will not cling to me."
Psalm 101:3

The following is a quote from the popular *Scooby Doo* cartoon show: "She was Wiccan. Wiccans are misunderstood; they are **not** witches and **are not evil**." In a 2010 episode, Velma becomes possessed by a demon. *Scooby Doo* has also shown witches, amulets, crystal balls, and astral projection. *Scooby Doo* is just a perfectly random example of what most Christian parents ignorantly deem as harmless/positive/acceptable entertainment for their children.

The Impact On Identity:

USA Weekend Magazine conducted a massive "Teens & Celebrities Survey" that surveyed 17,000 students in grades 6 - 12. In this survey, teens were asked what had been the main influence in their lives that had directed them to certain behaviors. 48% had chosen to drink alcohol, 47% had smoked cigarettes, 40% had taken drugs, and 25% had chosen to get pregnant out-of-wedlock mainly because of the influence of their "teen idol".(20)

USA Weekend concluded, "This generation of teenagers is not satisfied with merely staring at posters or even rubbing shoulders with their favorite stars -- they want to be them."(21)

MTV has stated, "At MTV, we don't merely shoot for the 14 year-olds, **we own them**."(14)

"Fyodor Dostoevsky predicted that at first art would imitate life, then **life would imitate art**, and finally, that **life would draw the very reason for its existence** from art."
Ravi Zacharias

"Do not be tricked by false words: evil company does damage to good behavior." 1 Corinthians 15:33

The Impact On Personal Development:

Research has proven that the more media teens consume, the less happy they tend to be. And those who are most captivated by media reported their academic performance suffered.(13)

An enormous amount of research has indicated that "mindless" television or video games may idle and impoverish the development of the prefrontal cortex: the portion of the brain that is responsible for planning, organizing, and sequencing behavior for **self-control, moral judgment,** and **attention**.(12) And we wonder why it seems that, all of a sudden, so many kids seem to have ADHD and ADD. (Media is not entirely to blame.)

Dr. Aric Sigman, after spending years of his life thoroughly analyzing 35 scientific studies, has found **15 negative effects** that naturally occur in adolescents as the result of watching television (and similar activities). These negative effects include **autism, obesity, premature puberty, diabetes, Alzheimer's, attention disorders, immune system damage, dementia, etc**.(19)

The Impact on Spiritual Development:

- 74% of church teens admitted to being spiritually and morally confused. 84% of those surveyed actually attended church **every** week.(15)
- 70-88% of students from "Christian" homes deny their faith before graduation from college.(16)
- **91%** of our "born-again" church kids say that there is **no** absolute truth.(18)

- Only **9%** of young people, under the age of 24, base their moral choices on the Bible.(17)

"There is a greater disconnect now than ever in the history of the church in America between what a 'Christian' young person says they are and what they actually believe."
Josh McDowell

The Solution:

The rampant sexualization of children and adolescents, the attacks on Christianity, the flagrant immorality, the pervasive education/ gradual desensitization of the occult, and all the rest of this degrading material has had a *huge* effect on the church of today. To "casually wade" through such waters without extreme per-cautionary measures (especially for children) is to wave a bloody foot in front of a hungry shark: there will be carnage. Dr. Aric Sigman's (author of the most extensive study on this topic to date) recommendation is to completely abstain from media that is even slightly questionable. If it doesn't glorify Christ then ban it! The Bible seems to fully support this recommendation and in many places seems to demand it. It is one thing to have to be in this ungodly world; it is another thing to bring the ungodly world into our own home to be viewed as "leisure and entertainment".

Please resist handing the one that you love dearly over to physical, mental, and spiritual handicaps that have been designed by godless men that are under the influence of Satan himself.

"And have given thee into the hand of brutish men -- **artificers of destruction**." Ezekiel 21:31b

"Blessed is the man that walks not in the **counsel of the ungodly**, *nor stands in the way of sinners,* nor sits in the seat of the scornful." Psalms 1:1

"But he that is spiritual judgeth **all** things." 1 Corinthians 2:15

"All things are lawful, but all are **not profitable**; all things are lawful, but **all do not edify**." 1st Corinthians 10:23

"**Regard with horror what is evil**; cling to what is right." Romans 12:9b

"For the rest, my brothers, whatever things are **true**, whatever things have **honour**, whatever things are **upright**, whatever things are **holy**, whatever things are **beautiful**, whatever things are of **value**, if there is any **virtue** and if there is any **praise, give thought to these things**." Philippians 4:8

Chapter 7
Is Music Moral or Neutral?

Even from just a casual reading through the Scripture, it is plain to see that God greatly values music. King Saul, while being oppressed by an evil spirit, would call David before him to play music for its ability to spiritually soothe. Music was almost always synonymous with worship in biblical times. King Solomon wrote over a thousand songs. The Bible includes a great deal of music in the book of Psalms. The questions that this article seeks to answer are relatively simple ones. Is music something that is apart from morals? Could it be neutral in a Christian's life? What is the sufficiency of Scripture for this?

Spiritual Development:

Now it is impossible to say that music is neutral in a broad sense because the Bible is clear that we will be judged by how we steward our time and resources. Therefore, one should expect to be judged by whether the music was beneficial, pointless, or harmful to their spiritual walk with God (and other personal developments as well).

Also, we will be judged on if we could have made even better choices toward edifying ourselves. Now some would object, "Wait a minute. God isn't going to judge me in that great of detail!" However, Jesus has said, "But I say to you, that for every *idle word* that men shall speak, they shall give account in the Day of Judgment." Matthew 12:36 The Bible also says that everything we do is being recorded. Our degree of reward will depend on even the thought and motive that was behind every action (or lack or action). (1 Corinthians 3:10-15)

It is also true that music has a profound effect on emotions, depending on how the notes have been organized. One can feel worshipful, melancholy, creative, suppressed, depressed, hypnotized, and energized all from different musical arrangements. It is important to recognize that certain musical styles can foster emotions that are unbiblical. For instance, heavy rock music can easily cause one to feel superhuman and self-sufficient. God says that man's life is a vapor. God says that man is totally dependent on Christ. Does your family's music enforce that idea or actively oppose it?

"...the prudent man carefully considers his ways."
Proverbs 14:15b

Mental Development:

We will also be judged according to how well we steward our mental development because our body is the temple of God. "Or are you not conscious that your body is a house for the Holy Spirit which is in you, and which has been given to you by God? and you are not the owners of yourselves." 1st Corinthians 6:19 The Bible also says, "To whoever much is given, of him will much be required; and to whom much was entrusted, of him more will be asked." Luke 12:48b We will be judged by whether we preserved or squandered the natural abilities that God has given us.

Certain music has proven to be extremely detrimental to the brain's functions, and some music has proven to be extremely beneficial. The effects depend on the order that is present in the music. This order includes repetition and changes, certain patterns of rhythm, pitch, and mood contrasts, and musical frequencies being used. Rock and rap music's order (especially regarding its low-frequency repetition) has proven to have a harmful effect on the brain's critical functions. As a result, it has harmful effects on creativity, self-control, moods, memory, problem solving, etc. Essentially, there is a "dumbing-down" of the listener. The adverse effects are, of course, compounded with increased exposure. Therefore, this music should be consumed responsibly (if at all), and Christians should strive to grow out of all music that is harmful to their mind.

> "All things are lawful for me, but **not all things are profitable**. All things are lawful for me, but **not all things build up**." 1st Corinthians 10:23

> "Everything is allowable to me, but not everything is profitable. Everything is allowable to me, but **to nothing will I become a slave**."
> 1st Corinthians 6:12

Who is the artist?

Another question of morality arises when one considers the artist. "Blessed is the man that **walketh not in the <u>counsel of the wicked</u>, Nor standeth in the way of sinners**, Nor <u>**sitteth in the seat of scoffers**</u>:" Psalms 1:1 How could it be possible to obey this passage of Scripture and, at the same time, be passively entertained by godless lyrics that are sung by someone who is godless and wicked? It is not possible. This is but one of many scriptures that command against allowing wicked men/women (and false Christians) to have this kind of influence in our lives. Jesus effectively shattered the myth of neutrality in Matthew 12:30 with the following words: "He that is not with me is against me." People have one of two fathers: God or Satan.

"Do not I hate them, O LORD that hate you? And am not I grieved with those that rise up against you?"
Psalms 139:21

"An evil man is disgusting to the upright..."
Proverbs 29:27a

Lyrical Content:

We are instructed by God to take every thought captive to the Lordship of Jesus Christ. We are instructed as to how to do that in Philippians 4:8. "For the rest, my brothers, whatever things are true, whatever things have honor, whatever things are upright, whatever things are holy, whatever things are beautiful, whatever things are of value, if there is any virtue and if there is any praise, give thought to these things." Here we see that if we focus on the good, we will be rejecting the bad by default. A Christian is to measure their music by this standard. We cannot let something dwell in our mind without taking it captive. Philippians 4:8 is the standard by which to take it captive. If the lyrics include things that are not pure, holy, true, honorable, upright, virtuous, etc., then it is not fit entertainment material for a Christian. There is no neutrality in any area of life for Jesus is Lord over all things.

"The fear of the LORD is to hate evil." Proverbs 8:13a

> "Do not love the world, nor the things in the world. If anyone loves the world, there is no love in his heart for the Father." 1st John 2:15

These are just a few of many layers that clearly define music as being moral. Napoleon once said, "Give me control over he who shapes the music of a nation, and I care not who makes the laws." I hope that we have all just seen in this chapter that music's morality is far from being an unclear matter. Now there are some songs that could be debatable because they are not necessarily positive, but they do not have anything evil in them as well. Let each one walk in the Spirit in regard to those songs. However, that is usually not the kind of music that people attempt to question morality over. People usually try to stick a "gray tag" on music that is flat-out reprobate. They have a million-and-one ways to rationalize and justify away all of the wickedness. While addressing this issue, let us all be sensitive to the Spirit while being keenly aware of the nature of God.

> "The highway of the upright is to depart from evil:
> He that keepeth his way, preserveth his soul."
> Proverbs 16:17

Chapter 8
What In the World Is My Child Listening To?

The adolescents of this generation are facing a huge danger. The mainstream music of America is slowly corrupting this generation from the inside on out. Music has the power to draw people towards certain worldviews and sins. It can numb the mind, quench the Spirit, and sear the conscience. It is worth noting that the vast majority of music being sold in stores and played over the airwaves is some of the most depraved music that one could attempt to imagine.

"Mainstream" can be defined as something that is in agreement with the contemporary, popular thought. Every Christian should be quite aware that the "contemporary, popular thought of today" is a very, very far cry from Christianity. Mainstream music today is full of blasphemy, hedonism, materialism, perverse lifestyle choices, godlessness, etc.

As stated previously, Napoleon has said, "Give me control over he who shapes the music of a nation, and I care not who makes the laws."

Music has proven to have incredible power on the conscious and subconscious mind. Studies have shown that it can take up to seven years for song lyrics to leave one's subconscious mind. **"For as he thinks in his heart, so is he..." Proverbs 23:7a**

The question that I am posing to every single parent reading this chapter is this: Are you completely aware of exactly what your child is listening to? The vast majority of Christian parents think they know, yet they do not even understand the lyrics being played into their child's ears. What is needed is to look them up and read them. Also, browse the other songs that the artist has done. When a child becomes enthralled with a certain singer or band, they will inevitably seek to listen to all of their songs. Yes, it takes time and work to go through every song on an MP3 player, to then look up the lyrics, and then read them. You also might even have to google what certain lingo is referring to. You might not even know how to accomplish those tasks, but there is still a solution. Find someone in your church that will do it for you!

91% of young people do not even believe that there is any absolute truth.(1) Do you really think that your child is going to come to you and ask if the particular music is acceptable? Parents don't know what is "cool" and "in". Children don't think that parents understand what they are drawn to so why would they come to you?

In general, the common morality of America can be observed simply by browsing the top 100 song hits. These 100 songs (and mainly the top 40) are what is being played over and over (sometimes 20 - 40 times a day) on the air. And if they are not playing, then it is a song from last month's top 100 hits, or the month before that, etc. Here is a quick look at what is currently on this list of the top mainstream music as well as brief characteristics of the performer. It is my wish that you would just imagine what the lyrics of these songs are like. If your child listens to mainstream radio stations, then it is most likely that they have heard songs from these people.

- P!nk: Her music videos include lesbian activity and even a same-sex marriage ceremony. Mainstream radio plays her hits very frequently.

- Katy Perry: She also glorifies the perverse and has released a chart-topping song about discovering the lesbian within.

- Lil' Wayne: He glorifies Satanism, drugs, promiscuous sex, blasphemy, lust, crime, and materialism.

- Ke$ha: She glorifies feminism, the club lifestyle, and unrestrained sexuality. Her current top song includes direct blasphemy against Jesus Christ.

- Lady Gaga: She has recently stated, "I very much want to inject gay culture into the mainstream." Just imagine what her songs and music videos are like.

- Taylor Swift: Lyrics – "It's just wrong enough to make it feel right." "So why the hell don't you love me? Why the hell don't you need me?" "Living off of bar tips." Her, and many like her, main focus is on "love". 99% of the time however, it is actually about *lust* and *not biblical love.* It often glorifies dysfunction as well. Many parents are blind to the fact that their daughter's sexuality is being stirred up before its time for them to be getting married. Meanwhile, her mind is being filled with unbiblical notions of love.

These are just a few examples, but almost every mainstream singer glorifies these things or at least many of them. If it's mainstream, it is almost guaranteed to be very perverse. If parents could only but see the ways that these people (and many others) glorify these detestable things, they would surely be in shock. The music is steadily degrading the church because teens view it as a gray issue while parents are not being vigilant.

Solutions:

Get on their computer and check their music library. Get their MP3 player and browse through it. Get their CD collection and go through it. Get their phone (if it has music on it which many do) and look through it. Once you see what they are listening to, look up the song lyrics. Also view other songs by the same artist (because they inevitably will). See what radio station they have their radio set on and research the radio station. If you do not know how to do any of these things, you must search for help until you find it. Ask around until you find someone willing. Eventually you will find someone that will be happy to assist you in this.

Chapter 9
Is God Against Heavy Christian Rock?

Rock's history goes back much further than what the average person would guess. To be more exact, it originated thousands of years ago. Rock first came onto the scene amidst the Dionysus Cult's rituals and practices. Dionysus (also known as Bacchus) was the god of wine, fertility (sex), and ecstasy. He was associated with drunkenness, madness, and, of course, unrestrained sexuality. The Dionysian music was a central part of the cult's rituals and celebrations that would include activities such as spirit-provoking, trances, summoning, worship, demon possession, orgies, hypnotization, frenzies, chaotic dancing, and heavy drunkenness. The music itself was used to induce the trances, frenzies, spirits, and all else. There were also certain characteristic movements as well, one being very interesting in particular: the *backward head-flick*. Is anyone up for some good ole' fashioned head-banging?

Now we will begin to explore what we have happening today. Keep in mind that this music was designed to promote certain activities and has seemingly continued to be perfected for those exact same purposes.

First of all, it is worthwhile to notice that the name of the cult is still thrown around by the industry even to this day. Jim Morrison was dubbed "Bozo *Dionysus*" by either Lester Bangs or Lester Bangs' headline writer. There is LA's, *Dionysus Records*, and also the one-million-dollar-a-year company known as *Dionysian Productions*. The Beatles, Rolling Stones, Velvet, Led Zeppelin Patti Smith, Ramones, Sex Pistols, Nirvana, PJ Harvey, and Smashing Pumpkins have all thrown the word *"Dionysus"* and *"Dionysian"* around.

What is also interesting is the recognition of all the consistencies present from the Cult of Dionysus. It is also consistently made very clear of whom the heavy rock music glorifies.

Press Officer for the Beatles – "They're [the Beatles} **completely anti-Christ.** I mean, I am anti-Christ as well, but they're so anti-Christ that they shock me, which isn't an easy thing."[1]

Ozzy Osbourne – "I don't know if I'm a **medium** for some outside source. Whatever it is, frankly, I hope it's not what I think it is - Satan."[2]

David Bowie – "Rock has **always been** the Devil's music. . . I believe rock and roll is dangerous . . . I feel we're only **heralding** something even darker than ourselves."(3)

Gene Simmons - "That's what rock is all about - **sex** with a 100 megaton bomb, the beat!"(4)

Ted Nugent – "Rock is **the total celebration of the physical**."(5)

Jimi Hendrix, who is among rock's greatest guitarists, said, "**Atmospheres** are going to come through music because music is a **spiritual** thing of its own. **You can hypnotize people with music, and when you get people at the weakest point you can preach into their subconscious** whatever you want to say."(6)

Dr. Granville Knight - "There is no question in my mind about the **hypnotic** effect of these songs."(7)

John Fuller - "Rock music in particular has been demonstrated to be both powerful and addictive, as well as capable of producing a subtle form of **hypnosis** in which the subject, though not completely under trance, is still in a highly-suggestive state."(8)

Dave Roberts - "Heavy rock is body music designed to bypass your brain and, with an unrelenting brutality, induce a **frenzied** state amongst the audience."(9)

Daryl Hall – "The main purpose of rock and roll is **celebration of the self**."(10)

Dan Peters - "**Sex has been rock music's #1 message since the medium was born**."(11)

Little Richard, the supremely famous rock-star, has said, "**Some rock and roll groups stand in a circle and drink cups of blood. Some get on their knees and pray to the devil. Rock 'n' roll hypnotizes us and controls our senses**."(12)

    Did everyone catch those consistencies? It **contains frenzies, chaos, the glorification of self, spirit/demon provoking, hypnotic effects, unrestrained sexuality, false spirituality, and drugs**. Compare that with paragraph 1! It's all there: "Sex, drugs, and rock 'n' roll" as the old saying goes. These elements are a part of the lyrics, lifestyle, and discipleship of the rock music genre. Do you think that all this is coincidence? I mean, really! Satan clearly has had his hand on this musical genre since its very conception.
    Let's look at other factors now. It has been proven by multiple studies that heavy rock music has terrible effects on the brain's critical functions, immune system, and other areas of

health and wellness. The Bible (and creation) proclaims that God is a highly intelligent God. The Bible also says that wisdom and understanding is to be sought after and highly prized. Therefore, it should not be suppressed and oppressed because of a choice of music. The Bible also speaks of proper stewarding of our body because it is the temple of God. Another factor is laid out in 1 Corinthians 14:33a "For God is not a God of **disorder**, but of peace..." Therefore, this music is against God's very nature in more ways than one.

The Dionysus celebrations were about **frenzies and chaos**. Rock music today still is about frenzy and chaos; it is the very nature of the music. "God is a spirit; and they who worship him must worship him in spirit and truth." John 4:24 We are told to worship him in truth, and we know that he is not a God of disorder. Therefore, it does not make sense to believe that the chaos of rock music is fit for worshiping Him. Deuteronomy 12:4 is clear that we should not worship God in the same way that the pagans worship their false gods.

I believe that God will still use what is happening for his own purposes, but this heavy Christian rock is clearly not fitting for a person living in the light. "Ye cannot drink the cup of the Lord, and the cup of demons: ye cannot partake of the table of the Lord, and of the table of demons." 1 Corinthians 10:21 "And what agreement has the temple of God with idols?" 2 Corinthians 6:16a I believe that we are seeing a severe lack of ministries that are actually walking after the Spirit.

(It is not being implied that certain instruments are not appropriate to be used for worship. It is all about how the instruments are used. There is a fitting way to play them, and there are ways that are against God's very nature as we have seen.)

Chapter 10
Discerning Between "Christian Music" and Music that Truly Glorifies Christ

It is very important to understand the difference between a *self-professing* Christian band's messages vs. the messages of the *genuine* Christian bands. Young people are being sucked into the popular Christian bands that are played on many Christian radio stations. They take it for granted that what is being sung is truth. The Bible warns us to, "Beware of false prophets, who come to you in sheep's clothing, but inwardly are ravening wolves." Matthew 7:15 "For such men are false Apostles, workers of deceit, making themselves seem like Apostles of Christ. And it is no wonder; for even Satan himself is able to take the form of an angel of light." 2 Corinthians 11:13-14

It is also possible that these people are not even deliberate false teachers; perhaps they are just not spiritually-grounded well enough to be teaching. Now some may be thinking, "Wait a minute. We are talking about songs, not sermons." What I'm saying is that there is a sermon in every single song. Every song contains theology and doctrine. Some of it is false doctrine and bad theology. "Stay away from a foolish man, for you won't find knowledge on his lips." Proverbs 14:7 Instead of taking truth for granted when we listen to something, we must carefully analyze it in order to test it with God's Word.

It is also sometimes necessary to seek out information on a band's personal life. This is done just in case they might show fruit of living apostate lives. "For every tree is known by its fruit." Luke 6:44a False teachings are extremely popular today, and many have made their way into the church already. We must be students of the Word so that we can approve of what is acceptable in God's sight. Let us now examine some doctrine that has been accepted by an enormously large Christian audience.

The Case against P.O.D:

It's sad that P.O.D. is even mentioned in this chapter because they never even claim to be a Christian band. Nevertheless, many Christians believe them to be "Christian" just because they are "spiritual". They are definitely spiritual! They are just the wrong kind of spiritual. Even their album artwork has blatant pagan and satanic elements.

Wuv of P.O.D. tells *Rolling Stone Magazine*, "Just because P.O.D. is a spiritual band doesn't mean we adhere to any **one religion**. . ."[1]

Sonny of P.O.D. says, "We don't fit in with the conservative values of Christian America."[2]

Marcos of P.O.D. blatantly says, "To tell the truth, I don't even like the term Christian. . ."[3]

Spin Magazine says of P.O.D., "Wuv and the band have structured their lives around a spiritual belief system that cross-fades Christianity, **Rastafarianism**, and **Judaism**."[4]

America's Christian music consumers have clearly been making blind choices.

The Case against Skillet:

Skillet has been openly accepted by thousands upon thousands of Christian young people. One problem is that Skillet performs very hard rock music. This was already thoroughly addressed in a previous chapter. The other problem is that Skillet's theology and doctrine is worse than awful. It is unknown by me as to whether they teach falsely by accident or on purpose, but that is not the important issue for the consumer. The importance lies within the fact that they are teaching a false gospel almost every step of the way.

- Their song, "Rebirthing", describes a person screaming for God, desperately searching for God, wanting to break free from Satan, and suffocating inside the flesh. However, the song speaks of him as not being able to come despite these intense desires.

This theology is way off! The problem here is that the song is speaking about becoming "born-again" in a way that is contrary to how Scripture describes it happening. "But people who aren't spiritual can't receive these truths from God's Spirit. It all sounds foolish to them and they can't understand it, for only those who are spiritual can understand what the Spirit means." 1 Corinthians 2:14 The hypothetical sinner, described in this song as longing for the new birth, doesn't exist. He can't exist! While in our blinded, captive condition, we want nothing to do with God and his Kingdom! Unless God grants new life to our souls, we will never seek him. Christians debate over "Efficacious Grace" vs. "Prevenient Grace," but besides all that it is abundantly clear that, apart from a gracious work of God, no one yearns for God. Their minds have been blinded by Satan (2 Corinthians 4:4, Romans 3:10-18).

- Their song, "Open Wounds", says that God (or a person) cannot stop them from falling apart because their self-destruction is all God's (or a person's) fault.

Scriptural doctrine says that personal responsibility is always a reality.

- Their song, "Awake and Alive", says over and over that we can do what we want because it's our life. Towards the end of the song, it is said that the heart belongs to God. Right after that, it is screamed once again that we can do what we want because it's our life.

This is a terrible doctrine of salvation and of the Christian lifestyle! Even Jesus himself said that it was not about self and his own life! These lyrics also imply that it is possible to give your heart to God and live for him, **and at the same time**, do what you want "because it's your life". Luke 9:23 says, "Then he [Jesus] said to them all: 'If anyone would come after me, he must **deny himself** and **take up his cross daily** and follow me."

The Case against Stryper:

Oz Fox (guitar), "To be honest, **Stryper wasn't where we should have been, spiritually speaking**. . . . I don't believe that the band, as a whole, was rooted like we should have been . . . There was sin happening in the band, and it shouldn't have been happening. **And the reason why it was happening is because we didn't know the Lord like we should have.**"(4)

Tim Gaines (bass guitar), "From the end of 1988 'till February of this year, I was drunk every day."(5) This band had performed for all three of those years.

Michael Sweet (lead vocals, guitar), "...that was kind of the **rebellious tour**, a **rebellious record** and we kind of vented a lot out of our systems on that record **for the bad and we all did some drinking and there are some things that happened that were the exact opposite of what we always stood for.**"(6)

Robert Sweet (drums), "As a matter of fact, **the band was one thing that was making us turn and walk the opposite direction from Christianity**, because, let's face it, **when you're out there playing <u>rock 'n' roll</u>**, and you're having a real good time doing your own thing it's not that you hate God or anything — <u>**you just don't want to think about Christ, because what he does is he exposes a lifestyle**</u>. <u>**If you're doing something you like doing, and God says**</u>

not to do it then you're not going to pay attention."(7)

Stryper has toured with White Lion and WASP (We Are Sex Perverts). Oz Fox even named himself "Oz" because of an obsession with Ozzy Ozzborne. He also lists himself as "Ozzie."

Syncretization with the world:

We can all rest assured that there are a *few* good Christian artists out there. Sadly, they are *far* from being the majority. The majority of the Christian music genre is just like the world. Amy Grant has played Joni Mitchell. Johnny Cash has played Danzig, Beck, and SoundGarden. 77's has played Led Zeppelin. DC talk has played the Doobie Brothers, Beatles, Jimi Hendrix, Nirvana, and REM. Audio Adrenaline has played Edgar Winter. Point of Grace has played Earth, Wind and Fire. Jars of Clay has played Ozzy Osbourne. Holy Soldier has played the satanic Rolling Stones. Deliverance has played Black Sabbath. No need to find bad theology in their songs because many of them are playing songs from heathen bands! I am not saying that all these bands mentioned are apostates. I am just pointing out the syncretization with the world that is occurring.

Steve Camp, a *CCM* artist, published a 107

Thesis to expose the false teachings that were rapidly emerging in the *CCM*. He also said, "We are producing a generation of people that 'feel' their God but do not know their God." The following is a portion of his insightful thesis.

- Thesis #7 – "We fail to glorify Him when we speak of God out of our own vain imaginings or **recreate Him** in our own image; instead of honoring Him by how He has revealed Himself through His holy Word."

- Thesis #31 – "For if in our worship we **pervert the truth** about God. If in our music we **distort His doctrine**, we distort a right view of Him. If in our song we **misrepresent the Scriptures**, we **misrepresent the Savior**. And if in our ministries we **twist His truth, we dishonor His character**."

- Thesis #41 – "Christian music, originally called Jesus Music, once fearlessly sang clearly about the gospel. Now it yodels of a **Christ-less, watered-down, pabulum-based, positive alternative, aura-fluff, cream of wheat, mush-kind-of-syrupy, God-as-my-girlfriend kind of thing**."

May we all be extremely vigilant in choosing who we allow to speak into your life through the medium of music. These artists usually say, "I'm a Christian," but it takes more than that empty statement to actually live and believe like one. Many people are beginning to believe the lies in some "Christian" songs and are being spiritually deceived. May God help his church to be aware of the lies that are so prevalent in today's culture.

> "Be vigilant, watch. Your adversary the devil walks about as a roaring lion seeking whom he may devour." 1st Peter 5:8

(No artists mentioned in this article were mentioned for the purpose of condemning them to hell, listing them as currently unrepentant, or forever unworthy of teaching anybody anything. They were included merely to illustrate the nature of much of the Christian music industry, as well as, to show how easy it is to be deceived if one has not done the proper research.)

Chapter 11
The Sufficiency of Scripture for Videogames

This intent of this chapter is not to condemn videogames as a whole. Its intent is to warn of their dangers, as well as, to give the sufficiency of Scripture regarding their usage. Videogames, much like other entertainment, I believe, can be consumed responsibly; however, this would be an *extreme* rarity among the consumers.

The Dangers:

- Videogames prey on the man's built-in desire to take dominion. This can even be seen in their advertising: "All new worlds to conquer."
- The Bible says that where your treasure is, there your heart will be also. Today's young people have all their treasure in some videogame. The game is where all of their accomplishments exist. The games even leech from the rest of their life because the

gamer is constantly thinking about the game, even when he is not playing it.
- Games can distract from the real challenges of life, and they can also reinforce the popular, godless notion that "life is all about leisure". Biblically speaking, life is about work; it's not about games.

Recreation is about re-creating. Therefore, it is possible for many games to be wholesome. *But* once a videogame turns someone to isolation, it is no longer re-creation. A game's purpose should not be to lead us into a fantasy world where we are distracted from the real issues of life and from what really matters. Our priorities promptly become misaligned. Needless to say, this could not be considered "redeeming the time".

One of the many errors that the world teaches is that life is all about leisure and comfort. Hedonism is a death blow to Christianity in the person's life that seeks after it. Hedonism is the epitome of lukewarmness. The Bible says that we are strangers and foreigners on this earth. **Ephesians 2:11 says,** "For we are God's own handiwork, created in Christ Jesus for good works which He has pre-destined us to practise." It's not about you, and it's not about me! It's all about God's glory.

So that I am not misunderstood, I will

attempt to be clear. I do not believe that *all* videogames are evil *in of themselves* (content), but I would say the majority are. I believe that some videogames can be used to re-create. However, the danger to abuse them should be well-recognized. The average age of a videogamer is 34 years old, and they have been pouring their lives into videogames for an average of 12 years.(1) What does this tell you about our nation? What does this tell you about sinful man's tendency? We are so easily led astray.

Today in America, boys remain as children for much longer than any other time in history. They no longer grow up to be men. A study has found that 33% men, aged from 20-40, are still living with their parents. 25% of men, that have actually left home, keep a furnished room at mom's house just in case.(2) Because of similar situations, we have had to come up with the "myth of adolescence" to try to rationalize away this peculiar, pressing predicament.

1 Corinthians 13:11 says, "When I was a child, I spoke as a child, I understood as a child, I thought as a child: but when I became a man, I put away childish things." Games are for children, they are not for men. The Bible speaks of the Christian man passionately pursuing God's kingdom. It does not speak of him passionately playing videogames (or constantly distracting

himself with things) that have no significance in the realm of eternity. The only time that is mentioned is in a manner of condemnation towards it.

How often do we see someone play videogames for hours, and then they read the Bible for 10 minutes at the most? What is happening here? We are spoiling young people's appetites for the Word of God with a steady dosage of videogames and other media. It's like constantly feeding a child candy. If you try to give them vegetables, they will not eat them. How is it that other countries' children crave fruits and vegetables? It is because their taste buds and appetites have not been spoiled. Do not expect your child to relish spiritual things when he is being fed a steady appetite of candy. He will not be able to appreciate the Word of God because his mind will be wrapped around a meaningless, pseudo reality that has absolutely no significance in the realm of eternity.

I am not calling for a ban on video games. I am calling for a re-alignment to God's Word. More specifically speaking, I am calling for a re-alignment to the priorities and principles that God emphatically gives us.

What Does The Bible Say?

> "Redeem the time for the days are evil."
> Ephesians 5:16

> "Now if any one build upon this foundation, gold, silver, precious stones, **wood, grass, straw, the work of each shall be made manifest**; for the day shall declare it, because it is revealed in fire; and the fire shall try the work of each what it is." 1 Corinthians 3:12-13

> "Not every one that saith to me, Lord, Lord, shall enter into the kingdom of heaven: but **he that doth the will of my Father** who is in heaven, he shall enter into the kingdom of heaven."
> Matthew 7:21

I am not implying that heaven's citizenship rests on whether one plays videogames or not. However, God's will is obviously extremely important. Do you think that it's God's will for people to sit on their rumps to play a videogame for <u>no other reason</u> than to distract themselves from the very short life that God has *entrusted* to them? If life is indeed just a vapor, then how much of that vapor can we afford to waste? The Bible speaks of life's briefness again and again. Yet how often do parents train their children to take for granted the preciousness of life by allowing them to frivolously waste away the time that God has entrusted to them? We can all learn much from The Parable of the Ten Talents. If God gives us time, he has entrusted us with that time. We will surely be judged by how we use that time. (Matthew 25:14-28)

In conclusion, Scripture teaches many things concerning this issue. Scripture speaks of stewardship, taking dominion, re-recreation (not distraction or isolation), growing to maturity, selflessness (instead of selfishness), and focusing on the things that are above; for only those things will have true, eternal significance. If any games can be used in that proper context, they are of God. If not, then they are against the will of God: (Colossians 3:1-2).

Chapter 12
A Glance at Media as a Whole

Much has been written about various specifics which will help us gain a deeper understanding of the "big picture". This chapter looks at the media through a slightly broader lens while sparing many of the details. Newly realized dangers will hopefully be brought to your mind, and you will receive much food for thought in this section. The main thing to understand is that the media could also be known as "the medium". This is because it is primarily a medium for two things.

- It is an incredible wealth of disciple-making information and materials that can aid you in your God-given endeavor.
- It is an umbilical cord from Satan himself to give you and your children a blood transfusion straight from hell. The ones that indulge in this have become blinded to the spiritual damage that is gradually occurring as they entertain themselves on things that are against God, and as they seek leisure over purpose.

"...you were unlike a prostitute, because you've scorned payment... Every prostitute receives a fee, **but you give gifts to all your lovers, bribing them to come to you from everywhere for your illicit favors... you give payment and none is given to you.**" Ezekiel 16:31b,33,34b

We **pay God's very enemy** (godless men, the corrupters of culture) to come into our homes, steal our children's hearts, and to sear our consciences.

Lupe Fiasco let loose a rather profound rant about *MTV* on his Twitter account. Lupe Fiasco is not a Christian, nor does he sing about things that honor God. However, he is not completely foolish about the media like many Christians are.

"Where are the honest critiques of cultural expression? For it's not about being RIGHT; it's about being HOT. Fame over self-awareness and virtue. Hedonism over self respect. Celebrity over cerebral. **A destroying force in our culture and society just like rest of the useless vapid spectacles that pour out of our TV's and radios. What are we supposed to be learning from you? What is your point? Do you have a point beyond corporate sponsored distraction? You're a materialistic shell of your former self that can only identify with celebrity pageantry and instant gratification. Corporate garbage**

pushing plastic lifestyles and wasteful, destructive behavior into the brains of the youth of the world."(1)

It should be noted that even Madonna does not allow her children to watch T.V.(2) She has been involved with media her whole life. She is aware of the effects, and even she is wise enough to protect her children. It is a sad day for the Church when an author of a pornographic book has more sense about what she should expose her kids to than the average Christian adult.

Susanna Wesley's definition of sin is always helpful when considering the implications of the influence that any given thing is placing on one's life. "Take this rule: **whatever weakens your reason, impairs the tenderness of your conscience, obscures your sense of God, or takes off your relish of spiritual things; in short, whatever increases the strength and authority of your body over your mind, that thing is sin to you, however innocent it may be in itself."**

The Boston Archbishop, Sean O'Malley, warned against the corrupt influence that the "glass idol" can have in people's lives. "The great spiritual sicknesses of our age and our culture come in great part from the extreme materialism and individualism of our age. Television is the pulpit of those influences."

Channel 23

"The T.V. is my shepherd, I shall not want. It makes me lie down on the sofa. It leads me away from the Scriptures. It damages my soul. It leads me in the path of sex and violence for the sponsor's sake. Yea, though I walk in the shadow of my Christian responsibilities, there will be no interruption, for the TV is with me. Its cable and remote control, they comfort me. It prepares a commercial before me in the presence of my worldliness. It anoints my head with Humanism and consumerism. My coveting runneth over. Surely laziness and ignorance shall follow me all the days of my life, and, I shall dwell in my house watching TV forever. Amen." (Author unknown)

    Am I concluding that the T.V. is inherently evil? NO! I'm just saying that almost everything on it is evil! We need to wake up and realize that the people in charge of the creation of these popular T.V. shows, movies, videogames, etc. are wicked people. What should we be expecting out of them? They are Satan's slaves according to 2 Timothy 2:26

    The stumbling block for some is the wholehearted belief that godless entertainment is a *right.* I doubt it that people who believed that would even make it this far in this book.

Therefore, I will not address that delusion.

Others say, "Well, the evil isn't really happening. It's just appearing to happen; it's all staged. Therefore, it is acceptable... Or it is, at the very least, neutral." Here's a big problem with that justification: "Abstain from all appearance of evil." 1 Thessalonians 5:22 Also, we must realize that the media is speaking lies. They are showing all of the sin without the consequences attached to it. David said, "He that practiseth deceit shall not dwell within my house; he that speaketh falsehoods shall not subsist in my sight." Psalm 101:7

I want to make sure that everyone understands. This is not about whether you should *have* a T.V. or not. This is about whether you should *use* the T.V. or not. I am perfectly aware that there are a few channels that are not wicked, and they also do not have wicked commercials. If you want to pay a bill every month just for those channels, so be it. But are you *able* to watch *just those* channels? Are you able to enforce that your children watch *only* those channels? Those are the key questions that should help you considerably.

I, myself, have a T.V., and I don't even watch it. Why would I? It's almost all trash! The commercials are trash, and most of the programming is trash. Should I watch some televangelist who's teaching false doctrine?

Wouldn't my time be better used listening to a sermon by someone that I can trust not to speak erroneous lies? "Stay away from a foolish man, for you won't find knowledge on his lips." Proverbs 14:7 As we all know, the internet is covered in this stuff too, but at least you have more of a choice to access something wholesome when online vs. T.V.

The last thing that I wish to address on this topic is the pseudo-Christianity that is so rampant in the media. I am speaking about a very specific penetrating force that is impacting the church today. Has anyone noticed that many unsaved Americans seem really "spiritual" at times? We have people talking about praying for you, and they have never even been to church. We have people that live in utter apostasy-ridden wickedness, yet they think they are going to heaven. The "free-grace doctrine" and universalism has had a bigger impact than many are aware of. We become accustomed to people professing Christ and calling themselves "spiritual", yet the fruit on the tree is bad fruit.

Let's dive into some "for instances". Justin Bieber recently released a song entitled, "Pray". So many Christians are just *so* happy! Don't they get it?! You can pray for the poor and needy all you want to, but *you* are *not* saved! Bieber has stated that premarital sex is morally acceptable and that the act of abortion is relative.(3)(4) "For as many as are led by the Spirit of God, these are the sons of God;" Romans 8:14 This "cultural Christianity" is all complete rubbishness that desensitizes us to what the Holy Spirit *really* produces; it also belittles Christ's saving grace. Once Bieber gets caught in bed with another Hollywood star, how does that make the Gospel look? How does that make the Church of Christ look? All this "spiritual" stuff is a knock-off: a pseudo! It turns *true* spirituality into something to be scoffed at. We should not be quick to embrace another's influence just because they make some sort of alluding profession.

How about a more blatant example? Kanye West put out the song, "Jesus Walks". Christians were so thrilled! One night, as I was speaking to a youth group about the Satanism in mainstream media, I even had one Christian youth ask me if Kanye was a Christian! Then, the youth pastor wouldn't even say that he wasn't! Are you kidding me!?! The rest of his songs (even on that very CD) blatantly glorify fornication, adultery, illicit drug use, idolatry, lust, perversion, and the like! His lifestyle, lyrics, ambitions, and affiliates are incredibly perverse! What has ever happened to a little thing called "spiritual discernment"? All this garbage heavily promotes antinomianism.

Oh, how about my favorite example? That would be Miley Cyrus: a.k.a. *Hannah Montana.*

She (and/or Disney) has spun a web of deception over so many Christian parents that it is simply unreal. How do those same parents feel now? Now that Miley Cyrus is doing "nude" photo-shoots for *Vanity Fair Magazine* (what an appropriate name for the magazine). Or how about when "intimate" pictures of Miley were leaked out onto the internet? Or how about when she had a stripper pole as a show accessory? Do you get my point? Christians have been so naïve at times (myself included) that we seem to be marks against the Gospel to the people that are watching us.

Okay, I could give more examples from music, but I'm going to now move on into visual media. I have seen many "Christian" movies that were heartily recommended to me by other Christians, and these movies were incredibly contrary to God's Word. One particular movie showed children sneaking around behind their mom's back. They were deceiving her and lying to her. Once they were caught, it's all just cute and funny because they deceived her for a little while. This is not God's view of children's deceit and manipulation of their parents.

Oh, how about movies like Evan Almighty? Almost everything about that movie's theology was blasphemous! Let's just be real for a minute. In the story, God appears to an unsaved man, He gives him a special task, and He works intimately with this man to complete it. However, there is no "coming to salvation". There is no need for forgiveness, nor is there anything even close to it. Of course, Christ is not even mentioned in the whole blasphemous movie. *As if* someone could come face to face with God (and His holiness) and still be the exact same person! That's a big crock of manure! Evan Almighty did an incredible job of leaving out good doctrine. They effectively put many unscriptural notions in the heads of many undiscerning Christians. We should not so readily accept all of this negative influence into our lives. 1 Timothy 5:22a says, "Lay hands hastily on no one..." "In order that we may be no longer babes, tossed and carried about by every wind of that teaching which is in the sleight of men, in unprincipled cunning with a view to systematized error;" Ephesians 4:13

For excellent media material that is good and well pleasing to the Lord, I highly recommend the utilization of the following media sources:

- Visionforum.com
- Sherwoodpictures.com,
- Westernconservatory.com
- Bluebehemoth.com,
- Wallbuilders.com

- Jeremiahfilms.com

The above sources hold a wealth of various types of media: educational, entertaining, informative, instructional, etc. If you want to use media in a God-honoring way, you will probably never need more media than what those websites can offer, and the content is very excellent. Visionforum.com has an abundance of other types of products as well. (I am not affiliated with them in any way. I am merely their extremely satisfied customer.)

"Keep thy heart with all diligence; for out of it are the issues of life." Proverbs 4:23

"But Daniel purposed in his heart that he would not defile himself…" Daniel 1:8a

"I will set no vile thing before my eyes. I hate the deeds of faithless men. They will not cling to me." Psalm 101:3

Chapter 13
The Peer Factor

1. God's design and purpose

God has *personally* designed a very special group of people: the family. He has placed them together so that when they look to one another, they are all in different places and can learn from each other. The parents are told that they must, in some aspects, be childlike. And for the children, the whole childhood experience should stretch to the goal of reaching maturity. *Ideally*, the child naturally has very good examples since his parents are who he/she spends most of their time around. The child is able to be spiritually preserved while being brought to maturity.

2. What is commonly occurring?

Satan has gotten most young people to absolutely disrespect the one who has been down the road and has much to teach them. Satan has also trained the older to look down on the younger. They should be looking at them as a disciple to bring to God, but the younger one ends up being despised or disliked.

Generally speaking, the young people of today are only looking to those who have the same short view that they do. They are only looking to the people who are making the exact same decisions that they, themselves, are making. A track record of benefits and consequences is obviously absent as well. This is all done with an attitude of "my parents just don't understand me or what I go through". Usually, the only time that the young people are looking to the older is when they are all traveling down the very same path of destruction.

> "Foolishness is bound up in the heart of a child;"
> Proverbs 22:15a

Let's all just honestly assess the situation for a moment. For the most part, parents are spending very little time discipling their kids. Peers are doing a phenomenal job of impacting the lives of other peers, and the discipleship that is taking place is extremely detrimental. Of course it would be! It's outside of the design of God.

In 1965, parents spent approximately 30 hours a week with their kids. By 1985, the amount of time had fallen to 17 hours.[1] Now, the number has fallen to a mere 3.5 minutes of "meaningful conversation" per day.(2) To make matters worse, the average American parent spends close to six hours every week just shopping!(3) Discipling someone takes time, but Americans just don't seem to have the time anymore. In most cases, it is because our priorities are backwards.

How is this peer influence happening? First of all, it is happening because it is filling a void in society. The void consists of parent's lack of involvement in their children's lives. It is primarily being filled through the avenues of mainstream media (T.V., movies, etc.), social media (Facebook, YouTube, MySpace, etc.), and, of course, from direct communication with friends.

There has been a great increase in the communication with friends through the increasing number of teens with cell phones, laptops, texting, etc. Teens with phones averaged nearly 2,900 texts per month.(4) That is an increase of 566% just in the last two years! People that text 120 times a day are 350% more likely to have had pre-marital sex. Hyper-texters were also more likely to have been in a physical fight, binge drink, use illegal drugs or take medication without a prescription.(5)

I am not calling for a ban on technology; I am calling for the proper use of technology. Is it necessary use? Or is it just giving Satan more stones to throw? What should the boundaries be? This must all properly considered as one weighs in what the technology is most commonly used for. The average Christian parent would fall apart at the seams if they were aware of what was taking place on their child's Facebook account, cell phone, laptop, etc.

3. Should I trust all of the friends of my child?

74% of teens *admitted* to being spiritually and morally confused. 84% of those surveyed actually attended church *every week*.(6) 91% of Christian youth do not believe that the Bible is true.(7) If so many of them are confused and worldly, and if 9 out of 10 are leaving the church, then what are the odds that your child has friends that will be a good influence on him? Parents, please be extremely wary of their associates.

Another study has shown that of 1,000 teenagers, 76% would go far enough sexually to feel experienced and to not feel left out.(8) One parents asked another parent, "Don't you trust your boy to be all alone with a girl?" The other parent replied, "Of course I don't trust him with that. Grown men, who are more spiritually mature with families to lose, cannot be trusted in that way. I trust human nature. I trust the Bible when it tells us to 'flee youthful lusts'."

The average age for sexual intercourse is 15 for girls and 14 for boys.(9) Religious-conscious girls are **only** 14% more likely to be virgins than nonreligious-conscious girls.(10) Barna Research also found that almost 50% of churched youth believe that "**everything** in life is negotiable, and that it is **morally acceptable** to do what is right in your own eyes."(11) That statistic has since risen dramatically.

> "Lot...pitched his tent towards Sodom." Genesis 13:12b

> "Don't be deceived! Evil companionships corrupt good morals." 1 Corinthians 15:33

> "He who walks with the wise grows wise, but a companion of fools suffers harm." Proverbs 13:20

4. What are some of the results?

"Peer dependence" is quickly bred as the child subjects himself to so much peer influence. Peer dependence is the fear of man; Proverbs 29:25a says, "The fear of man brings a snare." It is a shame that adolescents (children) are embarrassed to *even be seen with their own parents* for fear of what their peers will think. It is an extremely disgusting element of our American culture.

Peer dependence is what pushes many adolescents toward desiring the popular name brands. Once again, it is all centered on the fear of man and finding your identity in other people's perceptions of you. "For they loved the praise of men more than the praise of God." John 12:43

Peer pressure often leads to bad decision making. "The king was grieved, but because of his oath, and because he didn't want to back down in front of his guests, he issued the necessary orders." Matthew 14:9 I have seen people do some incredibly stupid things. Time and time again, it was a friend or a group of friends that had put the individual up to it.

Peer pressure *can be* a good thing *if* one has the right peer group. However, it's pretty slim pickings out there for any adolescent that is serious about God. Churched teens are very good at pretending the part. Hypocrisy is an integral part of almost all of the American, "Christian" young people's lives. I used to run in that crowd so I know what I'm talking about. The very few people that actually follow God are the outcasts in *most* youth group settings.

Today, it is expected for adolescents to experience a "rebellious stage". Well, what is this "rebellious stage"? I venture that it is almost nothing more than the simple sum of all the peer influence (and media influence) that had gradually accumulated combined with their fallen nature. They begin to get to the point where they are visibly rejecting their parents influence and instruction. They choose to incline their hearts to all the peer influence that they have had all their lives. Their hearts were gradually stolen, and rebellion was steadily bred. They are not rebelling against everything they have known. It is "selective rebellion". The peer influence and the media's influence progressively outweighed the parents' influence.

    I have heard parents say, "But I want them to develop social skills; they need to spend a lot of time around other peers for that." First of all, it has been proven that there is very little-to-no difference between the "social skills" of a child that is homeschooled vs. a child in the school system. Second of all, what kind of "social skills" do they think that a child can learn from a bunch of undiscipled, spiritually confused little brats? Do you want to know what children consider to be "social skills" that are in need of being developed? The skills of showing off and mouthing off! That's it! Pride and arrogance is at the top of the list.

    I went to a very conservative-Christian elementary school. I came there with an Associate's Degree in Lying; I left with a Doctorate's Degree in Deception. I also picked up my Master's Degree in Hypocrisy 101, as well as my Fornication Sex Education. Just because it is a conservative-Christian school doesn't mean that all of the students are conservative Christians! In fact, only about 5% were doing anything close to following God. I learned more evil and hypocrisy at that school then I care to describe.

The vast majority of the time, young peers just drag each other down. The younger is meant to be discipled by the older. I know some children that are good influences on each other, but those types of situations are unfortunately the rare exceptions, and it is only because their parents do an extremely good job of disciplining and discipling them.

> "Do not deceive yourselves: 'Evil companionships corrupt good morals." 1 Corinthians 15:33

> "...but fools despise wisdom and instruction."
> Proverbs 1:7b

Chapter 14
Culture's Most Popular Lies

Okay, we are going to change gears a little bit for this chapter. These lies that will be addressed always seem to get shot through the barrel of media and peers. There are so many of these lies that I could not possibly properly address all of them in this chapter. I have tried my best to select the ones that are the most prevalent and subtle. I have done so with the hopes of educating parents about what is happening. It is my hope that parents instruct their children regarding these things.

Jerry Bridges, a respected Christian author, has penned the following statement: "Many Christians have what we might call a 'cultural holiness'. They adapt to the character and behavior pattern of Christians around them. As the Christian culture around them is more or less holy, so these Christians are more or less holy. But God has not called us to be like those around us. He has called us to be like himself." It does not matter what front-row Joe or back-seat Pete does. We need our instruction straight from the Word of God. For young people in the church today, it has turned into a constant comparing-ourselves-among-ourselves-by-ourselves spirituality. That kind of spirituality leads to intense spiritual deception. Looking at each other, instead of looking at God's Word, is how many of these blatant problems have proved themselves surprisingly subtle in Christ's Church.

Let us now go through many deceptions that are taking hold of this generation.

Immodesty:

Today it is widely accepted that women's value is found in the attention that they can receive from men. Most of the female clothing in America is designed for that very purpose. If you don't believe me, I challenge you to research the history of American clothing. We are in a culture where there is a constant striving to glorify self by flaunting the body. A massive sexualization has taken place. Identity is found by how we look, what name brand we wear, our hairstyle, our shoes, our toenail coloring, and, most of all, how sexy we look. Paul said, "For to me to live is Christ." Philippians 1:21a

A contrast is helpful when considering how far we have come in such a short time. In the early 1920's, one would be arrested if they appeared in public dressed in a "modest" 21st century bathing suit. 90 years later, many *churches* have accepted the thong as being appropriate swimming attire. After all, no one likes being labeled as "old-fashioned". Movies and other media have popularized nakedness to the degree that if one challenges it, they are perceived as being strange or legalistic. We are in a culture that has completely turned itself to the sensual. We see this in all of the media, clothing stores, common places, and advertisements. The bottom line for American culture is that "sex sells".

Webster's Dictionary describes modesty in this way: "Behaving according to a standard of what is proper or decorous; decent; pure; and *especially not displaying one's body.*"(1) The bottom line is that God gave us clothing to *conceal* our body: not to *reveal* our body.

In a massive survey (with about 1,600 participants) for guys only, 85% said that all bikini's are immodest, and 93% said that miniskirts are immodest.(2) "He who is loving his brother, in the light he doth remain, and a stumbling-block in him there is not;" 1 John 2:10 "And he said unto the disciples, 'It is impossible for the stumbling blocks not to come, but woe to him through whom they come;" Luke 17:1 In a culture such as ours, girls need to be trained to ask, "Do my clothes say 'Christ, purity, and humility?' Or do they say 'fashion, sex, and pride?'"

When it comes to clothes, America says, "If

you've got it, flaunt it." That message is getting to the younger and younger age groups. In 2004, Miley Cyrus's younger sister began promoting a *children's lingerie* clothing line. How reprobate can America get?? Kids see this stuff everywhere: Movies, commercials, advertisements, peers, adults, internet, etc. Christians need to wake up and loudly shout, "The emperor has no clothes!" This issue needs to be attacked head-on in a young person's life because culture has firmly taken its stance.

Materialism:

Many Americans are completely out of touch with the rest of the world. We are spoiled rotten in many ways, and, as a result, we interpret the Bible in some funny ways sometimes. Many times when the Bible speaks of being blessed, it was speaking of being spiritually blessed. In our culture today, we have begun to interpret it strictly as being financially blessed. Now, being blessed can include wealth, but it is obviously not dependent on that.

Today's average parent's goal for their child is for them to be financially successful. Money is good, but it does not last. Should that really be the main goal for our children? Or should it be for them to get to heaven?

We have many warnings in the Word about putting too high of an emphasis on money, and this generation needs to learn these things because America is upside-down in this regard. Matthew 4:19 "And the cares of the world, and the deceitfulness of riches, and the lusts after other things entering in choke the word, and it is made fruitless." 1 Timothy 6:20 says, "For the love of money is the root of every evil; which some having aspired after, have wandered from the faith, and pierced themselves with many sorrows." The Bible also says, in Ecclesiastes 5:10, that the people who love money will never have enough to satisfy them.

Parents need to especially make sure that culture does not get the child off-course concerning materialism because this lie is very popular. Oh, that God would bless America with a generation that wholeheartedly believes that true success is only found in pleasing Him.

Hedonism:

The vast majority of Americans live for hedonism. Their main goal for life is to acquire much pleasure, comfort, leisure, luxury, and no pain. Needless to say, this is very much in conflict with the Gospel. Matthew 16:24 unapologetically says, "Then Jesus said to his disciples, If any man would come after me, let him give up all, and take up his cross, and come after me." Hedonism basically teaches that "if it feels good, do it; if it doesn't feel good, don't do it". This is the striving to gratify our selfish, fleshly desires. This is where we are at in case after case. For example, *The New York Times* has said that studies indicate that 75% of girls have had sex during their teenage years, with 15% having 4 or more partners.(3) The statistics for the boys are even worse.

Parents, I promise you, this is one of the biggest lies of today's culture. America worships the gods of pleasure, possessions, luxury, and comfort: Baal, Aphrodite, and Ashtoreth. This is almost all that one can see in the media. Statistics plainly show that hedonism is *the most popular* pursuit of today's culture.

America is clearly setting itself up to be judged harshly. In Abraham's day, Sodom experienced extremely harsh judgment. What were their sins? "Behold, this was the iniquity of thy sister Sodom: pride, **fulness of bread, and prosperous ease** was in her and in her daughters; neither did she strengthen the hand of the poor and need." Ezekiel 16:49

Hedonism says that it should be "your best life now". Having "your best life now" can only mean one thing: that you aren't going to heaven! Consumerism, lukewarmness, worldliness, and self's enthronement are the common byproducts of hedonism. Imagine a generation that loves their neighbor as their self. Imagine a neighbor who would give up comfort and luxury to help someone else. Parents, please teach your children these things well because culture is going to teach them the opposite.

Relative truth:

What is relative truth? At the very core, it is the belief that man is god; that we can define our reality, and that our definition of reality will be correct merely from our own assertion. In 2002, Josh McDowell said that 91% of our "born again" church kids claim that there is no absolute truth.(4) The Bible says that Truth is not a belief. The Bible says that Truth is a Person: Jesus Christ. If someone doesn't believe in absolute truth, they can't believe in Christ, and they definitely can't believe that the Bible is something to be taken seriously. "There is a way which seems right to a man, but in the end it leads to death." Proverbs 16:25 Yes, McDowell did say 91%! That is what your children are up against. The discipling that you are in the position to give them can make all the difference.

Consumerism:

"We must shift America from a needs culture to a desire culture. People must be trained to desire; to want new things even before the old has been entirely consumed. We must shape a new mentality in America; man's desires must overshadow his needs."(5) - Paul Mazer, a Wall Street banker working for Lehman Brothers in the 1930's.

Dear Readers, I hope that you are aware that America has been shifted in that way. Just take food for example. In 1995, America wasted more than 25% of their edible food. That's 96 billion pounds!(6) Do you remember the iniquity of Sodom? Part of it was their fullness of bread. At least 80% of humanity lives on less than $10 a day.(7)

Consumerism is just another way to exemplify self-gratification. We are bombarded with advertisements that teach us to desire, desire, and desire. We are trained to want our selfish desires for status, pleasure, comfort, and so on. James 4:3 spells consumerism out from God's point of view. "You ask, and don't receive, because you ask with wrong motives, so that you may spend it for your pleasures." America is breeding consumers, and they are using the media as their primary influence to do so. Expect your child to run into this problem in some way or another.

Individualism:

The individualist does not lend credence to anything that requires the sacrifice of the self-interest of the individual for any higher causes. An individualist enters into society to further their own interests alone. The family used to be a tight-knit household of people all working together. Now it is severely fragmented and segregated. Most young people are not, in any way, an asset to their family. This is because life, to them, is all about self. This destroys the unity and productivity of the family.

This is an ideology that the media pushes with full force. It's all about self-interest and self-worship. Matthew 16:24 says, "Then Jesus said to his disciples, If any man would come after me, let him give up all, and take up his cross, and come after me."

Individualism has also twisted the word "lust" to be known as "love". "I love you *for how you make me feel*" is the popular corruption. Yes, one usually benefits from love, but it is always defined as lust when self-interest is the primary driving force.

Lastly, God desires his people to be unified. God desires his people to be working together for a common goal and learning from one another. "Individualism" is exactly what the term sounds like it is.

Children are a curse:

Unfortunately, I will not be able to give this lie all of the attention that it deserves. All throughout the Old Testament prophets, there is lamenting over people losing sight of what the blessings of God are. The Bible says about a hundred times that children are a blessing. It also says about a hundred times that lack of children is oftentimes a curse. The Feminist Movement has changed the way that American culture views children, and this generation is going to be experiencing the worst of it. For the most part, Americans believe that children slow you down and are almost nothing except an unexpected, unwanted, and burdensome side-effect of sexual pleasure. God says that this could not be further from the truth.

This lie is propagated everywhere! During a televised interview, Sarah Palin actually referred to stay-at-home moms as being "Neanderthals". She also "supremely" stated, "I hope they evolve into something a bit more with it and a bit more modern."(8)

Today in American culture, if a woman says that she wants to dedicate her life to raising godly kids then she is scorned and looked down upon! People even accuse her of having no ambition! I am not saying that God does not call different people to different things. However, Scripture places motherhood as being the very highest calling, and everyone needs to exercise caution about referring to God's *blessing* as a *curse*.

> "Woe unto them that call evil good, and good evil; that put darkness for light, and light for darkness;

that put bitter for sweet, and sweet for bitter!"
Isaiah 5:20

False sentiment:

Today in America, we are trained to feel sympathy without coupling it with action. We are always seeing a gut-wrenching story in the news, a bum by the road, or a picture of an orphan child. We experience this false sentiment for but a moment, and then we get on with our lives.

Many reflective thinkers have concluded that emotions are meant to spark action. They are a primary driving force. If emotion is not coupled with action then we train ourselves to always separate the two. Since we are Christians, it is true that emotions should be subject to the will instead of ruling over it. However, it is proper for emotions to propel proper action. We must be wary of feeding ourselves a diet of false sentiment. Nothing is wrong with "feeling" for a person, but if there is no action, then what eternal good was that shallow empathy? Sadly, complacency has become commonplace in America.

> "Behold, this was the iniquity of thy sister Sodom: pride, **fulness of bread, and prosperous ease was in her** and in her daughters; **neither did she strengthen the hand of the poor and need.**" Ezekiel 16:49

Americans are trained to be this way. We can feel sorry for someone in the news, yet we do nothing for our own neighbor. Sometimes we don't even do anything for our own brother in Christ. This is something to be aware of because it is becoming more and more widespread. Satan seeks a people who have either shut their hearts to pity altogether, or people who will not take action after feeling the false sentiment of emotions with no action. "For God so **loved** the world **that He gave**..." John 3:16a

Evil is interesting:
Today, young people have been cleverly deceived into thinking that evil is interesting. Various media is always profiting from peoples interest in evil. Romans 16:19b says, "**I would have you wise to that which is good, and simple concerning evil.**" This goes back to the principle that is taught in Philippians 4:8. It is my hope that you teach your child that evil is mundane, and that godliness is what's truly interesting.

The "Here and Now":
It is most likely that any lie would stem from one common problem: we have become too distracted and enamored with "the here and now". Colossians says that we should be focusing on the things that are above. Jesus tells us that our very top priorities should be seeking His Kingdom and

His righteousness. Does that sound like Christ's Church today?

Americans are very good at passionately pursuing their best life here on this earth. If you ask someone what they do for God, many would ignorantly reply, "Umm… I go to church 2 times a month, and I pray once in a while." Are you kidding me!?! Matthew 24:12 says, "And because of the abounding of the lawlessness, the love of the many shall become cold." They grew cold because they were focused on the "here and now"; they were being swayed by many lies because they had not grasped firmly to the Truth.

Let's face it; there are tons of distractions today. Most children growing up in the church today do not know what God expects of them. This generation does not count the cost as Christ urged us to do. The majority of today's generation is either antinomian or agnostic. There are so many false doctrines and competing allegiances in America that everyone is forced to choose between destroying them and giving their life away to them.

What is the solution that God has given us concerning all of these cultural lies? "Don't be conformed to this world, but be transformed by the renewing of your mind, so that you may prove what is the good, well-pleasing, and perfect will of God." Romans 12:2 The renewing of our mind keeps us from being conformed to this world. How do we renew our mind? It is renewed through the reading, the studying, the understanding, and the application of God's Word.

Is this what today's generation of children are doing? Sunday School can only do a miniscule amount. It technically amounts to nothing when it is compared to the culture's discipling influence.

Teachers have the lowest amount of influence in a child's life. It is the parents that have the most influence. It is interesting that there is no command in Scripture that is directed at any kind of teacher that address the discipleship of children. These commands are always directed at the parents. God has given them the most influence, and apparently He expects them to utilize it. Parents that are purposely utilizing their influence have proven that there is only one sensible way of training a child in the way of righteousness.

> "All who have meditated on the art of governing mankind have been convinced that the fate of empires depends on the education of youth."
> Aristotle (384 - 322 BC)

> "Train up a child in the way he should go, and when he is old he will not depart from it." Proverbs 22:6

Chapter 15
Biblical Solutions

The Bible instructs parents over and over to be actively discipling their children. Proverbs has many such examples. Today, most fathers are not leading their families in the studying of God's Word. Very few are even seeking out God's principles in order that they, themselves, may live by them. Many seek success *outside* of the home instead of *inside* the home. This is true for a great deal of mothers as well. Instead of finding their fulfillment from serving God by parenting their children, they let the daycare, the babysitter, the public school, the T.V., or the after-school programs do it. Yes, *sometimes* life might have seasons that bring undesirable situations and/or consequences. However, let us never lose sight of what is ideal: God's original design. When those things are taking over the discipleship process, I urge you to beware. No one can disciple them like you can.

Today, most Americans find their identity in the career that they hold. We easily forget that if we have children, then that is our career. This is a major problem that has seeped into our society. We have forgotten what our priorities should be. Meanwhile, they have been clearly laid out in God's Word all along.

When parents dedicate themselves to the discipling of their children, I believe that many curses will be reversed. First, get your children away from the pollution and the polluters. Second, turn them towards appropriate things. Third, actively disciple them and win their hearts. If you wait too long, it will be too late.

This book laid out many specifics that should be watched out for, but the key things to be dealing with are the heart issues that capitalize on things such as these. We must be wary of just merely laying out a list of prohibitions. Many prohibitions are derived from wisdom, yet the heart issues must always be addressed as well. Let your child's "heart extensions" speak to you about what their heart issues might be.

Much of what was addressed in this book has stressed a separation from cultural corruption. This could possibly result in a misunderstanding of my recommended manner of handling these issues. I do not believe that you should keep your child "in a closet" until they are old enough to be out on their own. I believe that there is much wisdom in Geoffrey Botkin's approach. He trained his children, from a very early age, to be constantly making observations from whatever they were looking at or hearing. He would do this as he was reading a book to them or perhaps watching a child's movie with them.

Once they got older, he would carefully expose them to certain elements of corrupted culture so that they could make observations about them. Discernment is obviously needed to decide what would be unfit for this exercise.

Geoffrey Botkin was able to use this method to educate his children about culture's corruption, teach them from God's Word, and let them exercise discernment under his supervision and guidance. Obviously, Botkin's method was not centered on "being entertained". It was centered on God's Word, discipleship, and developing discernment in his children.

May God bless you in your endeavors of winning the hearts of your children as you disciple them according to the Scriptures, as you protect them from corruption, and as you discipline their folly. Visit visionforum.com for materials to assist you in this crucial undertaking.

> "And he shall turn the heart of the fathers to the children, and the heart of the children to their fathers." Malachi 4:6a

> "Only take care, and keep your soul diligently, lest you forget the things that your eyes have seen, and lest they depart from your heart all the days of your

life. Make them known to your children and your children's children." Deuteronomy 4:9

"And you shall teach them diligently unto your children, and shall speak of them when you sit in your house, and when you walk by the way, and when you lie down, and when you rise up." Deuteronomy 6:7

"And, ye fathers, provoke not your children to wrath: but bring them up in the nurture and admonition of the Lord." Ephesians 6:4

"Fathers, provoke not your children to anger, lest they be discouraged." Colossians 3:21

"That they may train the **young women** to love their husbands, to love their children, to be sober minded, chaste, workers at home, kind, being in subjection to their own husbands, that God's word may not be blasphemed." Titus 2:4-5

"Do not withhold discipline from a child; if you punish him with the rod, he will not die. Punish him with the rod and save his soul from death." Proverbs 23:13-14

"For I have made him mine so that he may give orders to his children and those of his line after him, to keep the ways of the Lord, to do what is good and right..." Genesis 18:19a

Works Cited:

Introduction –

(1.) http://www.csun.edu/science/health/docs/tv&health.html
(2.) Barna Research http://www.barna.org/barna-update/article/5-barna-update/164-new-research-explores-teenage-views-and-behavior-regarding-the-supernatural?q=witchcraft

Chapter 1 –

(1.) 2006. ChristiaNet.com. December 7, 2006
http://www.marketwire.com/mw/r...e_html_b1?release_id=151336).
(2.) (Christianity Today, Leadership Survey, December 2001).
(3.) ibid.
(4.) ibid.
(5.) (Internet Filter Review, 2006).
(6.) (Thompson, Sonya. "Study Shows 1 in 3 Boys Heavy Porn Users". University of Alberta Study, 5 March 2007,
http://www.healthnews-stat/com...0&keys=porn-rural-teens.)
(7.) (Market Wire. November 6, 2006. i-SAFE Inc. December 12, 2006 http://www.marketwire.com/mw/r...e_html_b1?release_id=180330
(8.) From http://www.internetfilterreview.com/internet-pornography-statistics.html - September, 2003
(9.) (Wolak, Janis, et al. "Unwanted and Wanted Exposure to Online Pornography in a National Sample of Youth Internet Users." Pediatrics 119 (2007); 247-257.)
(10.) From http://www.internetfilterreview.com/internet-pornography-statistics.html - September, 2003
(11.) (Lenhart, Amanda and Madden, Mary. Teens, Privacy, and Online Social Networks. Pew Internet and American Life Project, April 18, 2007
(12.) From http://www.internetfilterreview.com/internet-pornography-statistics.html - September, 2003
(13.) (Youth Internet Safety Survey, U.S. Department of Justice, 2001).
(14.) (Harris Interactive-McAfee 10/2008)
(15.) ibid.
(16.) (Girl Scout Research Institute, 2002).
(17.) ibid.
(18.) ibid.
(19.) (Thompson, Sonya. "Study Shows 1 in 3 Boys Heavy Porn Users". University of Alberta Study, 5 March 2007,
http://www.healthnews-stat/com...0&keys=porn-rural-teens.)

(20.)(National Attitudinal Poll, Common Sense Media, June 7, 2006, http://www.commonsensemedia.or...ws/press-releases.php?id=23).
(21.) U.S. Department of Justice, Post Hearing Memorandum of Points and Authorities, at l, ACLU v. Reno, 929 F. Supp. 824 (1996).

Chapter 2 –

(1.)(Michael Patrick Hearn edition; The Annotated Wizard of Oz, New York: Clarkson N. Potter, 1973)
(2.) (Anton LaVey, The Satanic Bible, New York: Avon Books, 1971, p.
(3.)(John Andrew Murray, "Harry Dilemma," Teachers in Focus; available from www.family.org
(4.) MTV news- http://www.mtv.com/news/articles/1584096/20080325/story.jhtml
(5.) The 2001 American Religious Identification Survey by the City University of New York
http://www.nytimes.com/2007/05/16/us/16wiccan.html?_r=1&scp=1&sq=wicca+fastest+growing+religion&st=nyt
(6.) Marla Alupoaicei- "Generational Hex" pg 6
(7.) The American Heritage Dictionary of the English Language
(8.) Harry Potter: Witchcraft Repacked by Jeremiah Films

Chapter 3 –

(1.) Google Adwords
(2.)"Pathways to Adventure", pg. 66
(3.)"Pathways to Adventure", pg. 70

Chapter 4 –

(1.)Washington Times of October 8, 1998, p.A8
(2.) American Family Association
(3.)AFA Journal 6/97
(4.) Daily Variety, 5/16/95
(5.)-Glamour, 8/9/94/B
(6.)Entertainment Weekly, 6/10/94; Daily Variety, 6/15/94
(7.)Daily Variety, 1/27/95; Newsweek, 2/20/95; Wall Street Journal, 3/30/95; Associated Press, 6/29/95/B
(8.)Out, 11/94
(9.)Newsweek 2/12/96
(10.)Daily Variety, 11/3/95
(11.)NY Times, 6/12/94

Chapter 5 –

(1.) http://twilightersanonymous.com/entertainment-weekly-twelve-stephenie-meyer-twilight-inspirations.html
(2.) ibid.
(3.) http://spesunica.wordpress.com/2008/12/10/interview-with-edward-robert-pattinson/

Chapter 6 –

(1.) Nielsen Media Research
(2.) Huston and Wright, University of Kansas. "Television and Socialization of Young Children."
(3.) A.C. Nielsen Co. (1998)
(4.) http://www.parentstv.org/ptc/facts/mediafacts.asp
(5.) Henry J. Kaiser Family Foundation: M2: Media in the Lives of 8- to 18-Year-Olds   (6.) www.turnoffyourtv.com/turnoffweek/TV.turnoff.week.html
(7.) A.C. Nielsen Co.
(8.) American Psychiatric Association
(9.) Greeson & Williams 1986).
(10.) http://www.parentstv.org/ptc/publications/reports/familyhour/exsummary.asp
(12.) American Academy of Pediatrics - Understanding TV's effects on the developing brain, Jane M. Healy, Ph.D. (From May 1998 AAP News)
(13.) Kaiser Family Foundation
(14.) (MTV is Rock Around the Clock, Philadelphia Inquirer, Nov. 3, 1982)
(15.) Study by Josh Mcdowell; statistics found in the book "Anchor Man: How a Father Can Anchor His Family in Christ for the Next 100 Years" page 65. Authored by Steve Farrar
(16.) barna.org
(17.) ibid.   (18.) Josh Mcdowell (2002)
(19.) http://www.wellness.com/blogs/DrLauraMarkham/294/childrens-tv-watching-linked-to-early-puberty/dr-laura-markham
(20.) http://159.54.226.237/06_issues/060521/060521teens_and_celebs.html
(21.) ibid.

Chapter 8 –

(1.) Josh Mcdowell (2002)

Chapter 9 –

(1.) Derek Taylor, Press Officer for the Beatles (Saturday Evening Post, Aug. 8, 1964).
(2.) (Hit Parader, Feb., 1978, p.24)
(3.) (Rolling Stone, Feb. 12, 1976)
(4.) (Gene Simmons of the rock group Kiss, interview, Entertainment Tonight, ABC, Dec. 10, 1987).
(5.) Ted Nugent, rock star, Rolling Stone, Aug. 25, 1977, pp. 11-13).
(6.) *Life* magazine, (October 3, 1969)
(7.) (Dr. Granville Knight, cited by John Blanchard, Pop Goes the Gospel, Durham: Evangelical Press, 2nd ed. 1989, p. 20).
(8.) (John Fuller, Are the Kids All Right?, New York: Times Books, 1981)."
(9.) (Dave Roberts, Buzz columnist, Christian rock magazine in Britain, April 1982).
(10.) (Daryl Hall of Hall and Oates, interview with Timothy White, 1987, Rock Lives, p. 594).
(11.) (Why Knock Rock? P. 67 ")
(12.) Little Richard quote from 1974

Chapter 10 –

(1.) (Rolling Stone, Dec. 14-21, 2000, p. 102)
(2.) (Spin Mag, Ocotober 2001, p. 88)
(3.) *Guitar Legends*, No. 37, p.28
(4.) (Spin, October 2001, p. 88)
(5.) (HM, Mar/Apr 97 #64, p.49)
(6.) (HM, Mar/Apr 97 #64, p.47 emphasis added).
(7.) On-Line Interview at
http://www.michaelsweet.com/interview.html
(8.) (RIP, April, 1987 p. 49)

Chapter 11 –

(1.) http://www.theesa.com/facts/gameplayer.asp
(2) http://www.dailymail.co.uk/femail/article-1201828/A-men-40-live-Hotel-Mum.html#ixzz18aIzRlFD

Chapter 12 –

(1.) http://www.ice-dotcom.com/2010/10/lupe-fiasco-spazzes-on-mtv-via-twitter/
(2.) http://today.msnbc.msn.com/id/9720314/ns/today-entertainment/

(3.) http://celebrities.beautyhill.com/justin-bieber-about-premarital-sex-and-abortion.html (4.) ibid.

Chapter 13 –

(1.) Source: William Mattox, "The Parent Trap." Policy Review. Winter, 1991. http://www.lifecoaches.org/Web/Research.asp
(2.) A.C. Nielsen Co. http://www.csun.edu/science/health/docs/tv&health.html
(3.) http://www.mainstreet.com/article/smart-spending/study-americans-shop-1-full-week-year
(4.) Common Sense Media
(5.) Kaiser family foundation http://www.dailymail.co.uk/health/article-1328062/Teenagers-text-120-times-day-times-likely-sex-peers.html
(6.) Study by Josh Mcdowell; statistics found in the book "Anchor Man: How a Father Can Anchor His Family in Christ for the Next 100 Years" page 65. Authored by Steve Farrar
(7.) Josh Mcdowell (2002)
(8.) http://kenbirks.com/outlines/moral-excellence-3.pdf
(9.) ibid
(10.) ibid.
(11.) 1994 study done by Barna research

Chapter 14 –

(1.) 1983 version of Webster's dictionary
(2.) Alex and Britt Harris' Modesty Survey— http://www.therebelution.com/modestysurvey/
(3.) http://books.google.com/books?id=kFBaP1TMnmYC&pg=PA285&lpg=PA285&dq=pleasure+college+students+survey+mcdowell&source=bl&ots=qmwGmnaps3&sig=J6DqnFc1UbcQYvB3Ktb5oyUyiQY&hl=en&ei=pwtcTejhHYGClAfQgM3jCQ&sa=X&oi=book_result&ct=result&resnum=1&sqi=2&ved=0CBYQ6AEwAA#v=onepage&q&f=false
(4.) http://www.abideinchrist.com/selah/nov6.html
(5.) the century of self documentary
(6.) According to a 1997 study by US Department of Agriculture's Economic Research Service (ERS) entitled "Estimating and Addressing America's Food Losses
(7.) (Shaohua Chen and Martin Ravallion, World Bank, August 2008)
(8.) http://www.youtube.com/watch?v=1OPF6HZMA5g

Made in the USA
Charleston, SC
02 April 2011